Foundations of Moral Decisions

a dialogue

Foundations of Moral Decisions

a dialogue

Thomas M. Olshewsky

University of Kentucky

WADSWORTH PUBLISHING COMPANY

Belmont, California   A Division of Wadsworth, Inc.

Philosophy Editor: Kenneth King
Production Editors: Vicki Friedberg,
    Deborah M. Oren
Managing Designer: Cynthia Bassett
Designer: Wendy Calmenson
Copy Editor: Elaine Linden
Cover: Cynthia Bassett

Printed in the United States of America

1 2 3 4 5 6 7 8 9 10—89 88 87 86 85

ISBN 0-534-03409-8

Library of Congress Cataloging in Publication Data

Olshewsky, Thomas M., 1934–
    Foundations of moral decisions.

    Bibliography: p.
    1. Ethics—Addresses, essays, lectures. I. Title.
BJ1012.O44   1985   170'.42   84-7248
ISBN 0-534-03409-8

To
my mother and my father,
who taught me early
the values of making my own decisions;
and
To
my wife, Judith,
who now shares decision-making tasks,
practical and moral, with me

Contents

Preface

THIS DIALOGUE AIMS to provide a new alternative for beginning ethical inquiry. The usual approach to moral philosophy is along one of two tracks. Either one begins with systematic formulations in ethical theory, usually by reading such great thinkers as Aristotle, Kant, and Mill, or one begins with the morally controversial issues of the day, usually by reading collections of essays by contemporary authors on such topics as war, violence, hunger, abortion, euthanasia, racism, and sexism. The former track often seems tedious and irrelevant to the beginning inquirer. Why worry about these issues and formulate them in such abstract, complicated ways? Also, the formulations often are linked to related issues about knowledge and reality. Those not already schooled in philosophical issues find they do not understand these systematic relations, much less appreciate them. The latter track leads into thickets of controversy where the writers often seem to take for granted that we all start out with common assumptions about what is fundamentally good and bad, right and wrong; or where they suppose no reasonable treatment of such assumptions, common or not, is possible. They often fail to answer the questions, Why do reasonable and informed people disagree on matters so crucial to their lives? And how can anyone come to satisfactory resolutions of such disagreements? For the novice, each track presents substantial, if not overwhelming, impediments to entering into the inquiry.

What alternative does this dialogue offer? *First*, it begins with a dramatic context in which thinkers with diverse views must come to some reasoned resolution of their disagreements. *Second,* the characters do not present systematically formulated theories, but rather achieve their own understandings of foundations for moral decisions through attempts to critically resolve their differences. Thus, there are pointed answers at every step of the way to Why these issues? *Third,* because the characters must make their positions understandable to one another in terms that people who don't share their positions can understand, they will be more understandable to the novice inquirer. *Fourth,* because the characters must respond to criticisms from differing perspectives, readers can gain not only some sensitivity to the strengths and weaknesses of each perspective but also some appreciation for why reasonable people disagree on such fundamental issues. *Fifth,* because the characters in the dialogue increasingly are able to trace logical implications for the foundational issues and for practical resolutions of moral controversy, readers get some models for their own beginnings in formulating a critical perspective on foundations of moral decisions. Indeed, what the dialogue form offers throughout is an invitation to readers to participate in the dialogue as fellow inquirers.

The dialogue, then, explores problems and perspectives through the critical exposition of the characters' attempts to find a common ground for decision making. In their *first meeting,* they explore preliminary questions of egoism (What obligations, if any, do I have other than the pursuit of my own individual desires?), of relativism (To what extent, if any, are moral expectations anything more than individual habit and social custom?), and of emotivism (How, if at all, are moral claims more than the expression of feelings about an issue or the prescription of a kind of action in relation to an issue?). The characters also explore their understanding of moral responsibility and the relation of punishment to responsibility. These explorations begin to reveal perspectives on goals and standards for moral action. In their *second meeting,* each is able to begin to expose the principles he or she supposes underlie moral action and thus to lay a basis for moral decision. They are also able to give some account of those principles in terms of their understandings of human nature and to give some critical appraisals of the similarities and differences among them. In the *third meeting,* they explore the relation of moral issues to social, legal, and religious considerations. The *fourth meeting* exposes differences in practical implications drawn from each theoretical orientation and the theoretical difficulties each orientation confronts in implementing moral decisions. Although these explorations do not produce a common foundation for moral decisions, they do produce mutual understanding that makes the task of cooperative decision making more workable. In the course of seeking that mutual understanding, they have explored many of the principal problems and perspectives of traditional ethical theory, and hopefully they will have made them understandable to the readers as well.

This dialogue is a beginning discourse about foundations of moral decisions, not an ending one. None of the characters begins the discussion as a moral theorist, and each ends with further problems to wrestle with. As students engage with the characters in critically exploring the issues, they will likely come to "take sides" with one or another and come to see how what he or she says about one issue has implications for a number of the others. The questions at the end of each meeting are calculated to encourage that kind of engagement and systematization. Insofar as this happens, students will become a part of the dialogue. Whatever perspective one takes up, I hope no one will lose appreciation for Gwen's sensitivities, for David's principles, for Roger's practicality. I also hope all will maintain a critical grip on the problems and pitfalls of their own positions as they come to articulate the advantages over the alternatives.

I hope this dialogue will prove challenging to the professional as well as accessible to the novice. Most doctors, lawyers, and ministers have sufficient background to enter into the dialogue at the level that Gwen, Roger, and David themselves did, and some may hear in their voices familiar echoes of Aristotle, Mill, and Kant. I also hope such readers will find some novel formulation or pertinent insight that will make these characters seem more than just echoes of traditions.

My primary audience has been the novice, however. Wherever possible, I have avoided technical jargon and appeals to traditions, leaving these matters for discussion in the suggestions for further reading at the end. Because so many issues are taken up in very rapid fashion, I have tried to provide reviews, summaries, and diagrams within the dialogue to help readers get their bearings. The questions at the end of each meeting can serve not only to elicit the readers' engagement but also to offer them a summary of the issues dealt with in that meeting. The marginal notes that accompany the dialogue are a kind of running synopsis of the conceptual interactions of the characters. They may be used as a tool to summarize or review a meeting after reading it and as a guide to relevant parts of the dialogue as readers attempt to relate their answers to those given by the characters in the dialogue.

This dialogue has been used effectively for the first part of an introductory ethics course, either accompanied by class discussion based on the questions in the text or accompanied by lectures that more systematically explore the issues raised in the dialogue. Treatments of practical problems have then been taken up against this background of competing theoretical perspectives. An equally fruitful follow-up might be a critical reading of classical texts in ethical theory against the background of problems exposed in the dialogue. Both of these plans can be implemented using the annotated bibliography at the end of the dialogue. Those engaged in professional or medical ethics courses may also find this dialogue an accessible theoretical preliminary to the discussion of the particular moral problems dealt with in those more specific areas of study. It may in a similar way serve as a prologue to social and political philosophy courses or even to courses in sociology and psychology that deal with moral issues.

In bringing this dialogue to you, I received many helpful suggestions, critical insights, and encouraging words from friendly supporters. Pat Harris and Fran McFall typed a draft that made preliminary uses of the dialogue workable in the classroom, and Linda Bowers put it into a form acceptable for copy editing. Kenneth King, Debbie Fox, Debbie Oren, and Vicki Friedberg, with their combination of editorial acumen and enthusiastic encouragement, made final touches less of a drudge than they usually are in such a project. Robert Ashmore, Marquette University, and John J. McCall, St. Joseph's University, in remarkably constructive spirit, suggested pedagogical aids and stylistic clarifications and noted some substantive flaws, providing the final version with refinements it would otherwise lack. David Black and R. Jeffrey Burkhardt tried out an earlier version in their introductory ethics classes, and they both continue to engage in the dialogue with me. Jeff suggested extensive revisions in a preliminary draft and has continued to make helpful editorial notes throughout the dialogue's development. David Wilson and Drew Litzenberger contributed more than just their medical sensitivities, and Phillip Shepherd offered his legal expertise. Last, and first, Judith not only cheerfully endured the presence of Gwen and Roger and David in the corner of our bedroom for a summer but also entered into the dialogue with them, to the benefit of their nurture and development. To all of these people, many thanks.

Foundations of Moral Decisions
a dialogue

The Characters

Gwen Martin, *a physician*
Roger Shepherd, *a lawyer*
David MacGregor, *a chaplain*

The Setting

The dialogue takes place in a hospital in a medium-sized city in mid-America. The time is approximately the present. The discussions occur over four meetings. The coffee breaks in the middle of the first three meetings are for the benefit of the audience as well as for the participants.

The First Meeting

THE SCENE IS Gwen Martin's office, where she and Roger Shepherd are already in the midst of heated discussion.

GWEN: I don't see why they set up this committee this way. Doctors have been regulating their own morality since the time of Hippocrates. Why do we now need some ethics committee made up mostly of people who don't know what it's all about?

Who is best able to decide moral matters?

ROGER: Anyone who has ever read the Hippocratic oath knows what *medical* morality is all about. It's about protecting the doctor and his profession. Take the Karen Quinlan case, for example. That got to be such a blown-up affair because the doctor refused to remove the life-support systems. Do you suppose he did that because of any moral concerns about the worth of the patient? Or even about prohibitions against "euthanasia"? The morality of a good death had nothing to do with it. He was making moves to cover himself from legal action.

GWEN: Well, the lawyer in the case wasn't much better. He was up for public office, and making political hay out of the situation. Even Karen Quinlan's parents seemed to vacillate on the issue. It seems as if they wanted to get off the moral hook by getting someone else to make the final decision. At least the physician in charge knew something about the medical cir-

1

cumstances of the case and was able to make some practical judgment on the basis of them.

ROGER: But that's exactly my point. Doctors make a *practical* judgment, but what that really means is they're figuring out ways to serve their own self-interests; in doing so they're constrained only by legal or institutional rules. Of course, lawyers do the same thing. Everyone does. Everyone has his own set of values, and sometimes they conflict with other people's, like the Quinlans and Dr. Morse, the physician in the case. You can't expect people to act the way they're supposed to unless you put legal restrictions on them. The hospital administration knows this; that's why they not only put a lawyer on this committee but also made me chairman.

Morality is based on self-interest constrained by law.

DAVID [having heard the last remarks as he entered the room]: I don't want to butt in, but I'm shaken by what I hear, if I understand it correctly. You seem to think, Roger, that everyone is just looking out for himself. You think there isn't anything to morality except what law requires.

ROGER: I don't see anything wrong with that. I do think that everyone is out for himself. That's not an issue of right or wrong. It's just the way we're wired.

DAVID: It's not an issue of wiring, Roger. We're each individual moral agents, made in the image of God.

ROGER: Oh, I don't doubt God. I also don't discount our individuality. I just think it is human nature to be self-seeking. Left to our own impulses and devices, we're out for all we can get for ourselves. Different people have different interests, and that makes them individuals, but everybody is out for his own interests.

Human nature is self-seeking.

DAVID: What you call human nature is traditionally known as original sin. It's by putting yourself first that the whole moral order gets out of whack. Man's *true* moral nature is one of benevolence and concern for others.

A counter thesis: True humanity is concern for others.

GWEN: It doesn't much matter whether you call self-seeking natural or sinful. But you both have a pretty negative picture of the human condition. Roger pictures human beings as acting like grasping infants all their lives. I assume, David, that you don't regard original sin as final.

DAVID: Oh, no! Quite the contrary! I see morality as the

Reason brings passions under control.

battleground of man's moral self against his sinful self. It's the task of reason to bring the passions under control. In a moral life, reason triumphs.

ROGER: Well, I don't like Gwen's way of characterizing things, but it's basically true. Grown-ups *are* grasping infants whose reason only serves them in solving the problems of getting what they want; but it doesn't make them any more moral than infants. That's why we need the restraints of law, and that's why you need a lawyer on this committee.

Roger claims passions are only controlled by the constraints of law.

GWEN: I think there is a good bit more to growing up than that. It isn't just getting reason together with passion. It's becoming a part of your society, learning to get along. By adopting customs and traditions, you find your way into the stream of life. Most of our moral life depends upon acting according to the habits and customs we acquire by becoming a part of society. We become more fully human by blending our interests with the interests of society.

Morality also depends on custom and habit.

DAVID: And what do you think guides you when your habits don't give you direction in some situation? You must agree with me that it is reason, since you so clearly reject Roger's idea of self-gratifying passions.

GWEN: I really don't think it's so simple as reason against passion. Roger and I were talking about the Karen Quinlan case before you came in. He said it was the insecurity of the physician that brought the case to court, but I think the case got so much publicity because it was such a difficult moral decision. The doctor didn't have to consider just the law and his medical judgment about how likely his patient was to recover. He also had to consider the value of her life and the burdens that her continued treatment put on her parents.

DAVID: That kind of complex situation is just what calls for the guidance of reason.

GWEN: Do you mean by that some sort of logical deduction, or some problem-solving technique, where you can feed data to your reason and come out with a solution? I doubt that any of us ever makes a decision like that. It's more like an intuition . . .

DAVID [breaking in]: Like a *rational* intuition?

ROGER [chuckling]: Or maybe like a woman's intuition?

GWEN [smiling]: Maybe like a woman's intuition, though I don't see it as a sex-linked characteristic. A moral decision isn't a case of rational insight or of divine revelation or even of some sort of moral sense. It's a case of things coming together in a decision-making situation. You don't consciously arrive at the conclusion on the basis of some reasoning process or moral sensitivity. But you do unconsciously bring to bear all of your relevant habits and skills and experiences in the decision situation. This is a survival technique of the human organism. We don't have time in a crisis to examine consciously all of the issues.

A third view: Moral decisions are made intuitively on the basis of habits and experiences.

ROGER: So there's no reason to prefer a woman's intuition over a man's. What, then, is your reason for preferring a doctor's intuition over an attorney's or a theologian's?

There may be a problem of conflicting intuitions.

GWEN: I don't always. Most doctors I know express themselves poorly and wouldn't even begin to follow some of your legal arguments, much less give the argument themselves. When a lawyer not only knows what the law is but also has good sensitivities for how to use it, we sometimes say she has good legal intuitions, don't we?

ROGER: Yes, I guess so.

GWEN: In the same way, when a doctor has good sensitivities about how to treat her patients, we say she has good medical intuitions.

ROGER: Sure, but what's your point?

GWEN: It seems to me that what is called for on an ethics committee like this one is the medical intuitions of doctors, not the legal intuitions of lawyers or the religious intuitions of theologians. I think in the Karen Quinlan case, the doctor was in the best position to make the right decision. If people want such decisions monitored, then that should be done by a group of doctors who can pool their professional judgments.

Medical intuitions are preferred to other professional intuitions on a hospital ethics committee.

DAVID: You've slipped off the track.

GWEN: How's that?

DAVID: We're not primarily concerned with medical issues any more than with legal issues. We're concerned with moral issues, with what is right and wrong, with what ought and ought not be done. In such cases, doctors don't seem to have more skilled expertise or more insightful intuitions than the rest of us.

But the issues are primarily moral, not medical or legal.

GWEN: Are you suggesting that we're all equally moral? You

make it sound like skills don't count in moral decisions. If that were so, one decision would be just as good as another.

DAVID: That's not at all what I mean. If we are going to make any sense of morality, then moral decisions can't be arbitrary. We may not be able to distinguish correct decisions from incorrect ones, but we can at least distinguish better from worse.

GWEN: Well, then, what did you mean?

DAVID: A person's professional skill doesn't guarantee his moral skill. A doctor's skill, for instance, may give him guidance to find the means to some moral end, but it doesn't help him determine what that moral objective ought to be. In his decision making, he may be more expert than those not medically trained in applying moral principles to medical situations—these situations have medical conditions to take into account—but his medical training gives him no specific guidance for what the moral principles ought to be.

Knowledge of means to a moral end is different from knowledge of moral ends.

ROGER: That clarifies the differences in our views on morality, David. You and I agree that the means are determined by reasoning processes. Here we would have to agree with Gwen: The doctor's knowledge and skill in a medical situation is going to make him most likely one to be able to figure out how to find the *means* to an *end*. Where we all seem to disagree is over how the ends are determined. You, David, say it's by *reason*. I say that doesn't fit with the self-seeking nature of human beings. People are driven by their passions, not led by their reason. Even for the more mature and the more sophisticated, the role reason plays is secondary. It helps them determine what means will best serve their own self-interest.

A proposal: Reason determines means; passions determine ends.

DAVID: I don't see how that leaves you with any basis for morality at all. With everyone out for himself, we might have *practical "oughts"*—what we ought to do as a means to gain our own ends—but we would never have any *moral obligations*—what we ought to do because it is right or good. We'd have craftiness but no genuine morality.

ROGER: If there are moral oughts, they are almost invariably negative. They tell us what not to do. They probably arise because, to protect itself, society needs a way to limit the means that individuals can use in pursuit of their own self-interest.

Moral oughts are negative limits on self-interest by society.

DAVID: Don't you see that runs counter to your belief that morality is based on individual self-interest? People can no longer act for themselves alone.

ROGER: No, what I said earlier was that people's ends are determined by their passion and that they naturally seek those ends. If we all tried to achieve our ends without restraint, we'd have chaos. What society provides is just those restraints. This is most obvious in the case of the law, with its means of enforcement. That takes us back to the role of a lawyer on this committee.

GWEN: It won't surprise you that I don't agree with either of you on the means-end distinction. I just don't think you can distinguish means from ends so neatly.

DAVID: Why not?

GWEN: You both talk about the distinction in the abstract, Roger on the basis of his very mean view of human nature, David on the basis of his very grand view of human reason. That's just not where decisions take place. They always take place in the context of a particular situation. Interests may influence and reasons may guide, but neither finally determines what the ends to be achieved will be.

Proposal: Means and ends depend on context.

DAVID: Then what do you suppose does determine the ends?

GWEN: My point is that there is no simple, abstract end people seek. The end is always conditioned by the circumstances in which people must make their decisions. Just as what counts as the relevant means will be determined by the end one has in view, what counts as a viable end will be limited by what means are available.

DAVID: That begins to sound pretty relativistic to me.

GWEN: I see nothing wrong in that, as long as you remember that the end is relative to something. Being relative is not necessarily being arbitrary or opportunistic. It's being considered in relation to something else. To call moral ends relative just means that they must be determined in relation to other things.

Moral relativity means that ends are determined in relation to other things.

DAVID: Such as?

GWEN: In the case we have been discussing, the doctor had to weigh his personal and professional commitments to sustain a human life against the economic and psychological needs of Karen's parents and the social and legal norms of our society.

DAVID: But, as you weigh these *relative* values, you have to rest your scales on something *absolute*. There has to be some standard against which your relative values are measured.

Relative values must be measured against an absolute standard.

GWEN: In a sense that is true, but not in the sense I think you mean. You seem to want some sort of universal moral standards set by reason. I don't think there are any. What we have are developed habits of individuals and customs of society that serve as standards to measure moral decisions in individual circumstances. These habits and customs develop out of what has worked in the past for resolving moral problems. Even these standards may be modified in a specific situation. That makes them less than absolute. It's the interaction between those standards and the conditions of the particular situation that produces the moral intuition I spoke of earlier.

Are there universal moral standards or only relative standards based on habits and customs?

DAVID: But don't you see there are human values and obligations that transcend situations and even cultures? What about the respect for human life?

GWEN: I remember reading in an anthropology book about a Pacific island society in which, when parents arrived at an age that might be called the fullness of life, it was the custom for their children to drive them up a tall palm tree, then shake the tree until their parents fell out and broke their necks. The religious justification for this act was that people entered the afterlife in the same bodily condition that they had just before their deaths in this life, and therefore death in the prime of life was a good.

Respect for human life may be shown in conflicting ways.

ROGER [breaking in]: There's a good example for you of religious rationalization of self-interest. When the parents become a drag on the economy, they bump them off.

DAVID [ignoring Roger]: That's an example of just the sort of moral principle that transcends cultural orientation.

GWEN: I don't understand . . .

DAVID: Let me try to explain by distinguishing *principles* for decision from *rules* for action. Principles are those ultimate values and obligations from which moral reasoning begins. Rules are those guides to action that are logically derived from the moral principles. They help us apply moral principles to specific situations in specific cultural contexts. The moral rules may be relative to a particular culture, but the moral principles from which they are derived are not.

Moral rules, which may be relative, are derived from principles, which are absolute.

GWEN: What in this case is a moral principle that transcends the cultural orientation?

DAVID: In this case there is both the value of human life and

7

the respect for parents. Both have to be understood in the context of a religious belief about a life after this one. On the basis of that belief, the principles of affirming life and of respecting parents are expressed in a rule about what you should do with your parents when they get to a certain stage of life. This isn't murder on this understanding. It is ensuring life everlasting. Should these beliefs change, the rules for action would also change, because the moral principles are themselves universal and unchanging.

ROGER [breaking in again]: The religious beliefs won't change, of course, until the economic conditions change, since it is the economic conditions that determine the religious belief. The belief is a rationalization that reconciles conflicting interests between living a prosperous life and living a long life in an economy that doesn't allow for both.

GWEN: I'm not sure Roger's analysis is right, but I still have problems with your claims about universal moral principles, David. If you have a moral principle that implies preserving the older generation as long as possible in one culture and abruptly terminating its earthly existence in another, isn't this a case of cultural relativity for morality?

DAVID: Not at all. I don't suppose doing away with one's parents is right in one culture and wrong in another. I think that the people in the second culture have made a bad application of moral principles based on a bad religious belief—or, as Roger would have it, on a bad resolution to an economic conflict.

Moral rules may be bad applications of moral principles.

GWEN: But how can you make such a judgment, other than from the perspective of your own cultural biases—social, legal, and religious?

DAVID: The powers of human reason are not limited by physical, social, or psychological conditions. They transcend those limits because they are based on a *logical order* to things rather than on a *causal order*. It is this distinction that lays the basis of moral freedom. Moral responsibility is the application of the logical conclusions from moral principles to practical circumstances. We are morally responsible to apply those rational conclusions to physical conditions as well as our understanding will allow.

Moral responsibility is the application of logical conclusions from moral principles to practical circumstances.

GWEN: Does that make the people in my story right in principle but wrong in application?

DAVID: Their *intentions* are right, but their *actions* are not the best ways to fulfill the intentions.

GWEN: So does the moral value lie with the *intentions* or with the *effects*?

DAVID: Surely those aren't our only options. We make moral judgments about persons and actions as well as about intentions and results. We also see that results of action are what we intend, so there is no easy separation of intentions from results of action.

It is difficult to separate intentions and actions in determining moral value.

GWEN: Well, what we can say, then, about moral responsibility in this case?

DAVID: We need to sort out two sets of questions. One has to do with what counts as right and wrong actions. The other has to do with how we hold the agents of those actions morally responsible. We may say that the act of someone who attempts murder and fails is morally reprehensible, whereas we may morally excuse someone if he kills someone without intending it. Sometimes killing someone by accident is not morally excusable; some ignorance is a matter of negligence.

Right actions must be distinguished from responsible agents.

GWEN: So, what do you do with the children that chased their parents up a tree?

DAVID: I would say that killing their parents was clearly wrong. But their understanding of that act was not to harm their parents but to help them into a happier afterlife. That understanding doesn't make the act any less wrong—the parents are dead, whatever the intent. It does, however, excuse them from the moral responsibility of the wrong.

Intentions determine responsibility.

ROGER [breaking in]: Do you mean they couldn't have done otherwise?

DAVID: No. Of course they could have done otherwise. They were acting of their own free will. In that sense they were responsible for their actions. They effected what they intended. They were also free to intend to do otherwise. They couldn't, given their cultural background, understand it other than they did. They did not *knowingly* murder their parents.

Responsibility implies a free will.

GWEN: So, you want to say that moral values and obligations are not culturally relative but that moral responsibility is?

DAVID: It doesn't sound quite right, the way you said it.

ROGER: It sounds to me as if you want to make people responsible for their intentions but not for the effects of their actions. Obviously, the intention is to produce the effects; the object or goal of the intention is the effects; the value lies with the effects, practically and morally.

DAVID: I don't think it makes sense to blame people for what they cannot understand or control. I think you can hold them responsible for what is in their power: the exercise of their own free wills. I don't always have the power to determine what the outcome of my actions will be, but I do have the power to determine my intentions. The intentions find their fulfillment in actions and their results, but moral responsibility has to do with exercising one's own free will. I'm not always free to effect what I intend, and I may not always be right about my intended effects being good, but I can always will to act with good intentions.

Intentions, not effects, are in our control.

ROGER: You talk about free will as though it was some sort of separate reality.

DAVID: You talk about motives to action as though we were physically determined, and Gwen talks about habits and customs as though we were psychologically and socially determined. The will must be free from causal determination in order to make sense out of moral responsibility.

GWEN: Well, whatever the theory, I need to be responsible to my own bodily functions. How about a fifteen-minute coffee break?

ROGER: Fine. Let's meet back here in fifteen minutes.

Coffee Break

GWEN: [entering the room with a cup of coffee]: Now that we've all had a chance to catch our breath and collect our thoughts, would one of you try to summarize where we've been before you go on with your debate over responsibility?

ROGER: Surely. We started with the question of who is best qualified to make moral decisions, but that led us pretty quickly to questions about how moral decisions are made. David and I seem to disagree about the roles of reason and passion in determining practical decisions. I think that desires determine ends and reason just tells us how to get there; David thinks that reason ought to limit and direct desires. This left me treating moral codes in relation to social laws and customs and David

Recap: Three views of the basis of moral decisions are reason, passion, and custom.

claiming that they should be based in the dictates of reason. Gwen, you came into the discussion with your claim that the reason–passion talk was too simple, that customs and habits had to be taken into account, and that the basis for moral decisions was an intuitive judgment based on all of these factors. That contention, along with your efforts to blur the means–ends distinction, was what got us into concerns with relativism. I don't think you and David ever got those concerns resolved before they led us into talk about moral responsibility.

DAVID: I'm a little surprised to find how many fundamental differences we have. We do seem to agree on some basic terms and distinctions, even though we may not agree on how they work in laying the foundation for moral decisions. We all distinguish means from ends, principles and rules from practice, reason and reflection from desires and passions. We also distinguish morality from practicality and legality, however it is that we see them related. Before the break, I was trying to work out a way to account for moral responsibility, what we expect of people, that distinguishes it from moral correctness, which kinds of actions are indeed right or wrong. This was in response to your claims about relativism, Gwen, but it opened up a new area of concern over what counts as moral responsibility and what sense we make of such claims. Surely, we can find some common ground in our understanding of moral responsibility.

Recap: All have in common distinctions between means and end, rules and principles, and the like.

ROGER: That depends on what you mean by responsibility. Responsibility can be simply the ability to respond. Punishment and blame are not ways of paying back for past wrong acts so much as ways of attempting to prevent future wrong acts. People are responsible for their actions if they are able to respond to such deterrents. It's this ability to take into account the rewards and punishments that are the natural effects of actions that lays the basis for a person's sense of good and bad.

Responsibility is ability to respond . . .

DAVID: That's just not good enough. Plants have the ability to respond to sunlight. Do you want to call that being responsible? Dogs and cats respond to rewards and punishments. Does that make them responsible? Responsibility implies not only the ability to respond but also respond willingly and knowingly.

knowingly and willingly.

ROGER: You're right. My starting point is not adequate, but our definitions may be just different in degree, not in kind. To respond knowingly is to know how best to respond to conditions in order to fulfill desires. Human beings can do that better than

To respond knowingly & willingly is to make the best use of information to satisfy desires.

plants. To respond willingly is to make the best possible match between desires and the means for their satisfaction. Human beings can do that better than dogs and cats. It's our ability to calculate our means and ends that sets us off from these other creatures and makes being responsible a matter of making the best use of the information available.

DAVID: Again, that won't do. Responding knowingly involves knowing what your duty is in the light of reason, and responding willingly is to be able to respond without restraint. That's basic to what it means to be moral. How can you ever get to issues of right and wrong on the basis of your understanding?

Responding knowingly and willingly is to know one's duty and to be able to act without impediment.

ROGER: Society adds a dimension of right and wrong by imposing laws and exacting punishment for those who break the law. Laws are necessary where the practical effect of bad actions is not direct and reliable enough to be a deterrent by itself. Society imposes laws to guarantee that rights and interests of its members will be protected, and it imposes punishment to make sure that people will obey the law.

Punishment is a social tool to increase responsibility.

DAVID: If I understand you right, you've turned the relation of punishment and crime on its head. Instead of punishing people because they are guilty, you claim people are *guilty* because they are *punishable.*

Then are people guilty because they are punishable?

ROGER: Something like that. In law we do indeed excuse people from punishment on grounds of their being unable to respond to the law and to the threat of punishment. When we judge them morally and legally incompetent, we recognize in them an irresponsibility that is different from those who could be headed off from doing wrong if they were to take account of the law and the punishments for breaking it.

DAVID: That may be some special, lawyer's sense of morality, but it's not what people generally mean. Ordinarily, for someone to be irresponsible he must act differently from what he knows is right. He's held blameworthy because he's done something wrong and could have done otherwise.

Responsibility is based on "could have done otherwise."

ROGER: I take it you mean "could have done otherwise had the conditions been different." Surely, you don't mean that decision making is unconditioned. To make sense of the world, we have to maintain that every effect has a cause.

DAVID: No, that's not what I meant. I meant that the person could have done otherwise in just those same conditions. The world of reasons is different from the world of causes.

The world of reasons is different from the world of causes.

ROGER: You don't need a different realm for reasons. Reasons for action are the desires that we have and the beliefs about how to fulfill them. These desires and beliefs are the reasons that serve as causes for action. They're not a different order of reality but simply kinds of causes that give an account of how human actions come about.

Roger maintains that reasons (desires) are causes.

DAVID: You and I understand reasons and causes quite differently. Desires play a part in reasoning about action, but they are not causes of action. They are not motives in the sense of the forces that move action. They are rather part of what we take into account in determining what to do through the reasoning process. This process takes place separately from causal conditions and is not explainable in causal terms. If the decisions are made according to reason, then they are truly free. They do not result from any psychological compulsion from within the person or from any coercion by circumstances, social or physical, from outside the person.

But David claims that desires don't move actions.

ROGER: I can't make sense out of that. You want to make freedom mean that people are not influenced by external conditions and not propelled by their own interests and desires. To me, freedom means being able to do something if I decide to do it. That's all that is required for practical freedom. You want to make the decision itself uncaused, detached from practical conditions. You claim the decision is rationally conditioned, but it sounds irrational to me. I don't think this is real freedom at all.

Freedom is being able to do something that you have decided to do.

DAVID: Well, my view of freedom may not be a perfect way of understanding things, but it at least makes some sense out of how morality is possible. Your view makes morality senseless. If we regard an action as morally blameworthy, we must suppose the agent was morally responsible in the very sense I have explained, that he could have chosen to do otherwise. With your view, it doesn't make sense to blame someone for doing wrong. Punishment as it is usually understood turns out to be no more than a harsh reaction to something over which the agent has no control.

GWEN: Why bother with blaming at all? I thought Christians believed in forgiveness, new life, and all that. Even if you can make sense of the idea "could have chosen to do otherwise" in the way you understand the world, I don't see how you can make sense of blame in the context of your Christian theology. If Roger sees punishment as the basis for deterring future crime, surely

Perhaps forgiveness is a better deterrent than punishment.

Jesus saw forgiveness as a basis for deterring future sin. Didn't he say, "Your sins are forgiven; go and sin no more"?

DAVID: He did indeed, but that is only a part of the picture. God is merciful, but he is also just. He maintains a moral order as well as a physical order to the universe. Forgiveness is accepting the sinner as a person but not accepting the sin as a right act. The sin throws the moral order out of balance, and punishment serves to put things right. Punishment is a way of paying back injustice to reestablish justice. *But justice requires paying back wrongs.*

GWEN: What I don't understand is how you can punish a sin without punishing the sinner. If someone steals and you cut off her hand, you may have made it hard for her to steal again, which is Roger's sense of punishment, but you have also diminished her life in important ways that have nothing to do with her wrongdoing.

ROGER and DAVID [simultaneously]: That's not my sense at all. . . . Come on! We don't punish people that way in our society anymore.

GWEN: We don't exact an eye for an eye, but we do exact a life for a life. By punishing murderers with death, or even life imprisonment, we take away their life because they took away the life of another. This doesn't give the murderer an opportunity to lead a new life if indeed he does repent. It does, I guess, prevent further crime, but only by preventing further activity of any sort. *Punishment cuts off the opportunity for a new life . . .*

ROGER: It isn't just the particular punished individual that we are attempting to deter from crime. If that were true, capital punishment wouldn't make sense. By punishing the offender, we are attempting to deter others from violent crimes.

GWEN: It's a notorious fact that stiffer penalties don't reduce the incidence of violent crimes. Most murders, for instance, are "crimes of passion." They are not planned for profit and take place usually within a circle of acquaintance that makes it highly likely that the murderer will get caught. It seems to me that such persons are not punishable on your analysis, Roger. The threat of punishment does not keep them from doing the crime. Yet you favor capital punishment on the pretext of prevention. *and does not deter serious crime.*

DAVID: Well, what do you propose as an alternative? Letting them go free?

GWEN: I'm afraid that I don't have a simple, practical

alternative to either of your conceptions of punishment, but I can tell you ideally what I think ought to be done.

DAVID: What's that?

GWEN: You said earlier that you thought someone wasn't really free if she acted contrary to reason.

DAVID: Yes.

GWEN: Well, I don't think that someone really is free when she commits a crime either. I think she either is not aware that it is a bad thing she is doing or she finds what she is doing preferable to her other options.

DAVID: You think that nobody does wrong of his own free will?

GWEN: I mean that no one intentionally does wrong, that each person always intends to choose the best course available to her. Some actions are based on ignorance or compulsion or coercion, but even in these cases the person involved usually supposes she is taking the best alternatives.

No one intentionally does wrong.

DAVID: But that would take morality out of the picture, because no one would be blameworthy for wrong action.

GWEN: Don't misunderstand me! I said that we don't intentionally do wrong, not that we don't do wrong. The ways in which we go wrong are what have to be corrected.

DAVID: Like what?

GWEN: Well, if it is a problem of ignorance, that can be overcome by education. This may require more than just giving information. It may require developing skills to do certain kinds of things or learning ways to alter habits and customs in ways of relating.

DAVID: This doesn't deal with blame for wrong action.

GWEN: In a way it does. When a person becomes aware that past ways of acting were wrong, she takes the blame on herself. If her blame is regret for past action and that strengthens her intention to act differently in the future, it is effective blame. If it is simply guilty feelings that amount to self-punishment, this is as debilitating as if someone else were punishing her.

Only blame that improves action is worthwhile.

DAVID: Then you don't think we ought to blame her—or him—or whomever.

GWEN: I don't think we usually blame people for their ignorance. What we usually do is blame them for refusing to overcome their ignorance.

DAVID: What you are saying, then, is that wrong action is either the result of someone's being coerced from the outside into the act or compelled from the inside by mistaken conceptions, by ignorance of the right action, or maybe just by moral weakness.

GWEN: That's right. So, if it's a matter of coercion, we need to change the social environment; if it's a matter of ignorance or mistake, we need to educate; if weakness of the will, we need to alter the psychological makeup of the person's character.

ROGER: Sounds like a lot of liberal, idealistic nonsense to me.

GWEN: I said it was an idealized solution to the problems of criminal action. I don't really suppose that our society has the economic resources or the moral sensitivities or the social and psychological skills to carry out the task. But we ought to be able to do better than put people into prison, where the most likely things they'll learn are ways to be more artful criminals.

Such total reform is probably not practical.

ROGER: Our job here isn't to reform society. Whatever the value of all this talk about responsibility, freedom, punishment, and so on, it doesn't do much for the task at hand. It hasn't gotten us very far in understanding how to resolve practical issues of social policy and individual interests as these problems confront this hospital.

DAVID: That's because we have barely scratched the surface of the fundamental questions about morality. We're just beginning to learn to talk to one another about these matters.

GWEN: We have such diverse opinions on almost every issue that it's hard for me to see how we can ever arrive at any agreement on any issue. If we have this much difficulty agreeing on the foundations of moral decisions, imagine what it will be like when we come down to dealing with real cases.

ROGER: I have other difficulties with this than superficiality or complexity. Gwen thinks moral issues are hard to talk about because people deal with moral decisions intuitively. I think the problem runs deeper. Because actions are motivated by feelings of self-interest, so-called moral judgments are really little more than expressions of those feelings.

Roger suggests the basic problem in dealing with moral issues is that moral judgments just express feelings . . .

GWEN: Are you saying that "This is good" means nothing more than "I like this"?

16

DAVID: If that's what you are saying, then there would be no real moral disagreements. If you say something is good, it means that you like it. If I say it's bad, it means that I don't. There's no disagreement between us.

ROGER: No, that's not what I mean. That would just be a shift from a claim about the object to a claim about myself; from the objective to the subjective. I don't think the expression "This is good" makes a claim at all. All it does is give expression to my attitude about something. It doesn't make a statement; it expresses a feeling.

DAVID: There has to be more to it than that, even from your perspective. Surely, when you say something like "This is good" to me, you mean to convey something more than your feeling, since you at least appear to be making a claim about the thing we are talking about.

ROGER: That's why I said the judgment was little more than the expression of my feelings. The "little more" is my hope to get you to share my feeling. I'm expressing my feeling and inviting you to try out feeling the same way toward the same object. If at first you don't feel the same way, I may give you "reasons" for feeling that way, but these amount to calling your attention to things about the object that might elicit the same positive attitudes that I have.

and are invitations to others to share those feelings.

GWEN: So moral disagreements, in your view, amount to differences in attitude that get in the way of pursuing your own self-interest.

So one may pursue her self-interest?

ROGER: Something like that. What appear to be moral claims are more like ways of persuading someone to think about things in certain ways, positively or negatively, so you can get the person's cooperation in pursuing your own self-interest.

DAVID: I don't think that works even for claims about value. There must be something about the object you are trying to persuade someone about that elicits your attitudes in the first place. The value has to be there in the object or you wouldn't ever get around to making expressions of your feelings about it. You value it because it's valuable; it's not valuable because you value it. . . .

A counterthesis: Values are objective; one values something because it is valuable.

ROGER [interrupting]: But you don't . . .

DAVID [refusing to be interrupted]: The important issue for

morality is not so much value as obligation. In the end, morality has little to do with what is valuable, and less with what we like, but with what we ought to do. Obligation is the crucial issue for moral consideration. You can't say that expressions of obligations make no claims. Obligations can't be reduced to expressions of feelings and attitudes.

Obligations make objective claims.

ROGER: I've already said my piece on obligations. I think they are strictly social restraints, they are set by convention, and they are best expressed in law. I think human action is always concerned with the worth of the object of action and that issues of obligation come in only as a social means of individual pursuit of those aims.

GWEN: Well, just to put my piece in, I think you have both split the world up into pieces in really bad ways. David wants a moral world separate from a practical world, and so splits obligations from values along those lines. Roger wants a private order distinct from a public order, with the one governed by the dictates of individual passions and the other by the expectations of social obligations.

ROGER: And what do you want, Gwen?

GWEN: I want a focus of morality on the worth of the person; on virtue and integrity that bind together value and obligation into a coherent whole. I want my head to stop buzzing with all the bustling confusion of this conversation. I want this committee made up of people who are trained as doctors and who feel and think with that sense of integration, so that I won't have to constantly struggle with people always coming at each issue from a different perspective.

Morality should focus on virtue and integrity that bind together value and obligation.

ROGER: Well, to take a page out of your own book, Gwen, you have to start in context from the conditions as you find them. What's given in this context is that the three of us are on the committee and I am the chairman. We can't change that. What we can do is figure out ways to get along and how to proceed to get our job done efficiently. We've already been over the moral foundations stuff, and we're beginning to go in circles.

GWEN: Since you're chairman, what do you suggest?

ROGER: That we proceed like a court. We'll review the facts of the case, take a vote, and I'll designate someone to write up an opinion that will rationalize the vote for public consumption.

DAVID: Now, Roger, you surely have listened to us long

enough to know that Gwen and I can't go along with that design. One of the things our discussion so far should have revealed is something of what we can and cannot tolerate.

ROGER: Well, what do you suggest?

DAVID: I suggest that we quit for today. Gwen is right. We're all saturated with bouncing our differences off one another. It takes a while to see how all this stuff fits together and where it leads. But I suggest we go on with it for a couple more meetings.

GWEN [breaking in]: Please . . . no more.

DAVID: Let's at least try to accomplish two things. One is for each of us to get clear what our own views actually are and how they fit together. You, Gwen, by your own confession, don't feel very comfortable or very adequate about saying just what the basis of your claims are. The other thing is to understand where each of the others is coming from in his views. This should at least reduce friction when we come to dealing with practical cases. I *hope* for another objective, but I don't expect it. I hope we may even come to some reconciliation, if not straight-out agreement, on at least some of the issues.

ROGER: I hate to waste the hospital's money and our time with this stuff, but we are into this as a long-term standing committee. It may be worth a couple of meetings to try David's proposal, just to make this a more congenial committee.

GWEN: I guess I can go along with another session or two. It may help reconcile me to the existence and the makeup of the committee, since as Roger points out, we're stuck with both.

DAVID: Things aren't in quite as bad disarray as you and Roger seem to think. Even our disagreement on free will and determinism hasn't been fruitless. Roger's arguments haven't convinced me that he's right and I'm wrong, but they have helped me understand how someone might hold his views. I didn't understand your arguments as well as Roger's, but I think I'm more sympathetic with yours. It's also pretty clear that there are direct lines of inference from these views to those we take on crime and punishment. I'll be interested to see if we can trace them further in our next discussion.

Philosophical disagreement can lead to understanding, if not acceptance.

ROGER: These issues don't seem to me to be very relevant to the job of this committee.

DAVID: If they are not, others are. One is that you and I are at odds, Roger, over how the aims, or goals or ends, of moral action are determined. On the social level, you say convention; on the individual level, you say feeling and desire. I maintain that if moral goals are not determined by reason, it is not a moral matter. You leave room for reason in determining the means to achieve ends, but think it has no role in setting the goals and aims themselves. I assume that feelings and desires are not relevant to determining ends.

Recap of differences: Are goals of moral action determined by social connections and individual desires, or by reason, or by the person using both thought and feeling?

GWEN: And I, of course, find them all relevant but in a different way. I think people deliberate about moral goals integratively and interactively. Decisions are made by the whole person using sensitivities and thought together. Feelings and reflections each play a part, but not exclusively.

ROGER: These differences probably have something to do with the different emphases we place on moral evaluation. Gwen wants to ask if the person has good habits and character and acts with integrity according to them. David wants to ask if the person had good intentions, if he arrived at his conclusions on sound moral grounds. I want to ask if the action produced good results, if it fulfilled the desires of the actor within the limits of society's standards.

Recap continued: Is moral evaluation based on habits and character, on intentions, or on results?

DAVID [writing as he speaks]: It seems we have covered even more than I first thought. Look, we can lay these perspectives out on a kind of chart. That will help us express our views more coherently.

	How are the goals of moral action determined?	*How are standards for moral judgments set?*	*What is the focus of evaluation of moral action?*	*What is the purpose of punishment?*
ROGER	By desires	By individual desires and social conventions	Results of action (worth of the object)	To deter crime
GWEN	By desires and reason interacting (?)	By the nature of the individual and the way society is constituted	Commitments and characters of actors (?) (virtue and integrity)	To rehabilitate wrongdoers
DAVID	By reason	By reason	Intentions of action (duty and obligation)	To pay back injustice

GWEN: This is a nice start, but I think we have a lot more to do in systematically describing and defending our perspectives. We also have to trace some implications for some moral problems so we can see what differences, if any, follow from the different perspectives to their practical applications.

ROGER: Let's meet twice more on these matters.

GWEN: I have one other concern that seems a side issue, but an important one. We have talked about sin and crime, but I would like to make sure that we don't confuse religious and legal issues with moral ones.

DAVID: That's a concern that may work itself out as we deal with the other matters. Let's just wait and see.

Questions for Reflection & Discussion

1. David and Roger have different understandings of the relation between passion and reason in making moral decisions. Which, if either, makes more sense to you, and why?

2. Gwen doesn't find the reason–passion distinction adequate. What does she offer instead? Is this better than what David and Roger suggest?

3. Roger sees social laws and conventions as necessary to control individual passions. Does that equate morality with legality?

4. Why does Gwen think it was the doctor in the Quinlan case who was in the best position to make the right moral decision?

5. Does David's distinction between means and ends serve to make his point that the doctor was not necessarily in the best position? How?

6. Roger wants to equate moral ends with practical ends. What are David's objections to that?

7. Roger maintains that moral "oughts" are invariably negative. Can you think of a counterexample (an example of some moral obligation that is positive and is not just the most practical way to achieve some further end)?

8. Gwen maintains that all aims or objectives, moral or not, are dependent on contexts. Can you think of a counterexample (an example of something good or right in itself, with no qualification by context or by conditions)?

9. Do you think David's distinction between moral principles and moral rules settles the question of cultural relativity? Why?

10. To meet Gwen's challenge of moral relativity, David distinguishes between moral permissibility and moral excusability, between

wrong acts and culpable persons. Do such distinctions meet the challenge?

11. David and Roger offer different interpretations of the meaning of the words "freedom" and "responsibility." Which interpretations do you find appropriate to moral responsibility? If you find both views appropriate, how do you make them compatible?

12. David and Roger have different understandings of the relation of reasons and causes in human action. Which model of human action do you find more workable for understanding moral action? Why?

13. Do the different senses of moral responsibility offered by Roger, David, and Gwen depend on their understanding of free will and determinism? If so, how? If not, why?

14. Do their treatments of crime and punishment depend on their understanding of free will and determinism? Explain.

15. The conversation takes for granted that there is some relation among crimes, sins, and immoral acts, but none of the participants ever spells it out. What do you suppose this relation is? (Are all crimes immoral? Are all immoral acts sinful?)

16. Roger maintains that "This is good" is only an expression of feelings. Does this imply that it is nonsense to talk about moral disagreement?

17. David maintains that you value something because it is valuable, not that it is valuable because you value it. Do you agree? What does this imply for the objectivity of values?

18. Gwen left off with the question of how to keep moral issues distinct from religious and legal ones. How do you maintain these distinctions or why do you prefer not to?

The Second Meeting

The scene is Dr. Martin's office, the next morning.

ROGER: I noticed yesterday, Gwen, that you used feminine pronouns when you spoke. Don't you think that is a feminist affectation?

GWEN: No. It's just the only thing I've been able to come up with that will serve as a defense against the male-oriented linguistic prejudices of our society. I've trained myself to speak that way so that I'm not usually self-conscious about it. Yesterday, I noticed that about the time feminine pronouns popped up in my speech, talk about men and mankind dropped out of yours and David's. You very cooperatively began talking about people and persons.

DAVID: I'm afraid you'll have to forgive me if I continue to talk of man and mankind. It's not only a well-established habit, but one that I think is backed up by good old-fashioned generic meaning. Then, too, there is something about the ring of phrases like "the good of man" that just can't be captured by the translation, "the good of persons."

GWEN: I'll try to accept your usage if you try to keep in mind "the good of women" as well.

DAVID: Of course. The good of all human beings. Given yesterday's conversation, it won't surprise either of you to find that I believe there is a good for all mankind. I've been thinking since our last meeting about how best to express it. The formulation I came up with is that the only unqualified good for man is a good will.

The only unqualified good for man is a good will.

ROGER: By unqualified here, I suppose you mean without conditions.

DAVID: Yes, in the sense that there is no "ifness" about it. Some things are good only as means to ends. These are the practical goods of tools and conditions to pursue our goals. Some things are expedients for a full life, like good health and good relationships. But the only thing that is good without qualification is a good will.

GWEN: And by good will, I suppose you mean benevolence.

DAVID: No. Benevolence is an important good. It's like good health in its contribution to a good life, but by being a contribution to something, it is dependent on conditions, and so is not unqualifiedly good. By good will, I mean willing what is right.

Good will is willing what's right.

ROGER: That sounds like you are saying it's good to do what is right. That seems so obvious that it's trivial.

DAVID: It is obvious, but it isn't trivial. It's obvious because it is implicit in our very understanding of morality. It's a kind of basic moral fact that everyone ought to do his duty. This sense of obligation has conditions when the goods to be achieved are tools for furthering other goals or when they are goods that preserve or promote a good life, but the obligation is unconditional for doing what's right. If something is the right thing to do, then there is no qualification on your obligation to do it. Good will isn't trivial because it can serve as a form for determining what you ought to do in a given situation. It is like a receptacle that is empty by itself but gives structure to the content that is poured into it.

The obligation to do what is right is unconditional; a form for determining what right action to take.

ROGER: What do you mean?

DAVID: You may remember my maintaining yesterday that God created a moral order as well as a natural order. Both orders operate according to the principles of reason. These principles include consistency and continuity. Part of our sense of causal law, or a natural law, is that things happen in the same way under similar conditions, and that events occur in temporal and spatial relation to themselves. This gives us our sense of coherence, of things hanging together in the world. The moral order must also be coherent, which means that laws that apply at one time and place also apply at another time and place and those that apply to me also apply to you.

Moral laws must be generalizable.

ROGER: So you want generalization for moral law in the same way as there is generalization for physical law.

DAVID: Not only want it. Must have it. Doing what's right is always to act so that the rule that guides your action could be generalized to all actors, could be a universal law. Anything short of that turns out to undercut the coherence that the moral order requires. When I will that my action be in accord with a universal law, I am trying to fit myself into the rational moral order. If that's not doing what's right, doing my duty, then nothing is.

Right action is fitting into the rational moral order.

ROGER: I can see how generalization works for physical laws. You notice regularity on the basis of repeated similar instances, and you then hypothesize that instances of this kind always work that way. Moral law, on your account, seems to be a result of willing and acting, not generalizing from observation. In the one, we are making a law to fit our world; in the other, we are requiring our world to fit the law.

DAVID: I don't think you are right about the way that physical laws work, but there's no point in getting off on that tangent now. The crucial point about moral law is not so much that everyone is required to do something as that there is a duty for everyone to operate within the bounds of reason. Maybe the rules of the moral law are more like rules of a game than they are like the regularity of physical laws. They set limits on what you can do, but they do not dictate what you can do. That leaves possibilities of play within the limits of the game.

Moral law is bound by the limits of reason, although not dictated by these limits.

ROGER: But in the case of games, rules are conventionally set as means to fulfill the goals of the game. They constitute the form of the game, and in that sense are basic; but they also serve as means to fulfill the goals of the game, and in that sense are instrumental, rather than good in themselves. So, if rules of morality are like rules of a game, then they are determined by convention and are not fundamental to the moral enterprise. I thought you maintained yesterday that moral ends were based on reason, and I know you maintained today that the only unqualified good is a good will.

DAVID: Maybe I can make it all clear with an example. My principle for a good will is that I should never act except when I can will the basis for that action to be a universal law. Suppose that I want to steal something. If I attempt to will stealing to be universal—that it's all right for anyone to steal whenever he wants to—then I come up with a rational absurdity. If everyone stole from everyone, then the very notion of private property would be undercut. That would mean the stealing itself would no longer make sense, since stealing takes for granted that there is private property. That's why it is a rational impossibility to will that everyone ought to steal.

Stealing, for instance, is not a good act because the basis for that act is not generalizable.

ROGER: It seems like you've practiced some logical sleight-of-hand here. You say you can't will that everyone ought to steal. It doesn't follow that you must will that everyone ought not to steal. Between ought-to and ought-not is the broad area of permissive behavior that you already suggested in your game analogy.

DAVID: You've misunderstood the conditions. Let me try again. The basic condition for my action being moral is that I be *able* to universalize the general rule for action, that it be practically and logically *possible* for anyone and everyone to act in this way. If I cannot make sense of it as a possible act for everyone, then I cannot actually do it morally. Because the rational conditions are the same for everyone, any person acting morally in the same situation ought to come to the same conclusion.

To be morally permissible, an act must be possible for everyone.

GWEN: Now you qualify universality in terms of situations. Does that mean you would recognize circumstances as a part of your formulation of the rational conditions? Certainly, this is true of physical laws. Water boils at 100°C, but only if certain conditions of air pressure and water purity are met. Are similar conditions relevant for moral laws? Suppose someone is in a situation where she will very likely die soon if she doesn't get something to eat. She's starving. Let's put her on a boat where the food supply for crew and passengers is gone, but there is food in the cargo. Let's also suppose that the boat's occupants are cut off from rescue by communication and transportation. The radio is broken and the engine is out of commission. So her choice is between starving or taking food from the cargo. Under such circumstances, wouldn't it be all right for anyone to steal?

How far can generalizations be qualified by circumstances?

26

DAVID: There are reasons why I'd have to say no. I'm sympathetic with the situation you describe, even though it's a contrived one. I'm sure that in real life there are many such difficult moral situations. But sympathy is not the basis for morality. We're dealing here with a slippery slope. If you start letting sympathies or other qualifications override the moral law, it's an easy slide to making your judgments about the rightness or wrongness of an action relative to time, place, temperature— even the idiosyncrasies of the actor. If you tack on enough conditions, you no longer have a generalization but merely a prescription for a particular act by this person in this situation.

Qualifications may be a "slippery slope" from generalizations to prescriptions for single instances.

GWEN: Qualifications and exceptions can always be carried too far. A law devised for one specific instance makes a mockery of the notion of law.

DAVID: Exactly. But where do you draw the line short of that final absurdity? We have no rule or guideline to determine when situational conditions have gotten too specific, and each of us would feel differently about where to draw the line. The only rational basis for judgment seems to be an unqualified rule.

ROGER: I'm not sure that absolutes are more rational than relatives. They are just easier to see because they are so clear-cut. Just because you don't have a clear-cut place to draw the line doesn't mean that people cannot approximate where the line belongs. Just as you don't have to lose all of your hair before you are said to be bald, something doesn't have to be unconditional before you can say that it's right. In Gwen's example, it seems more right to steal than to die of starvation.

Are absolutes more rational than relatives?

GWEN: I begin to suspect that David doesn't recognize relative values among rules either. Do you think that killing is more wrong than stealing, David?

Does morality admit degrees?

DAVID: Right and wrong actions, like true and false statements, don't admit to degrees in value in the way that good and bad do. A statement is not more or less true or sometimes true and sometimes false. Either it is true or it is not. Morally relevant actions are either right or they are wrong. We may find some wrong actions worse than others—we may blame their agents for them more—but they are not more wrong.

Right and wrong do not admit degrees, although good and bad do.

ROGER: But can't we treat right and wrong as more like accurate and inaccurate or adequate and inadequate? Sometimes we find answers to questions almost right, and we find calculations almost accurate. Why not actions that are almost right, or at least not as wrong as others?

GWEN: If you don't allow for some relative values, how do you justify your treatment of punishment as you described it yesterday? You make the penalty for murder greater than the penalty for theft.

DAVID: Wait a minute. You two are trying to make me deal with three different aspects of the issue all at once. It still is the case that even when something is almost right, it is wrong. Although one answer to a question may be closer to correct than another, I don't suppose that one immoral act is any more moral than another. It strikes me as odd to say that stealing is more moral than murder. On matters of punishment, you will remember that we blame actors, not actions. We blame them not just for their wrong actions but also for the bad effects of their wrong actions. Moral justice requires punishment in proportion to the degree to which the moral order is upset by the wrong action. Even though murder is no more wrong than stealing, greater harm comes to a person by taking his life than by taking his money. Even though premeditated murder leaves the person no more dead than a murder committed in a moment of passion, it involves more evil intent. It is the act that is right or wrong, but we take account of both intentions and effects when we evaluate the degree to which the moral order has been violated.

Some effects are worse and merit more punishment.

ROGER: Neatly sorted out, though I'm not sure that in everyday life we really do treat punishment that way. But you suggested there was more than one reason for rejecting Gwen's situational conditions on moral rules.

DAVID: Perhaps the best way to characterize my other reason is to distinguish the kind of knowledge we have of moral rules from the kind we have of situations. Gwen set up her example to make sure that the conditions would lead to starvation, but in real life we can never be sure that the conditions are what we judge them to be. In the case of Gwen's ship, the radio or engine might get fixed or the Coast Guard might come to the rescue. These are possibilities that can't be controlled for. The judgment that it is wrong to steal, however, because it is not dependent on circumstances, is free from such uncertainty. You can be sure about being right in your moral judgment even when you can't be sure about the practical results.

Moral judgments must be free of uncertainties of practical results.

ROGER: I still think I'd go for the best calculatable results.

DAVID: Let me give you another example. Suppose I come to your apartment late one night, obviously panicked, and tell you that someone is chasing me with a gun, trying to kill me. I ask you to hide me. What would you do?

Should one lie to save a life?

ROGER: I'd send you into the bedroom to find your own hiding place, and then I'd call the police.

DAVID: Soon after that, your doorbell rings, and you open the door, thinking it is the police. It turns out to be my pursuer, who threatens you with the gun, says he saw me come in, and wants to know where I am. What would you do?

ROGER: I'd lie without hesitation to ensure saving your life. Since he saw you come in, I'd tell him that you had been there but had gone out the back door just minutes before.

DAVID: And while you were doing this, suppose I had panicked again at the ring of your bell, had left your bedroom, and had actually gone out your back door. Your lie in an effort to protect me could turn out to be a contributing cause to my murder.

ROGER: What would you propose as the moral thing to do: to tell him the truth?

GWEN: You would have the option of remaining silent.

ROGER: The old sin of omission is better than the sin of commission stuff?

GWEN: I'm not sure it has much to do with sin one way or another. You have the logical alternatives of speaking the truth, telling a lie, or remaining silent. From your being morally obligated not to lie, it does not follow that you are morally obligated to tell the truth. You are obligated to tell the truth or remain silent. As a doctor, I have to sort out the difference between killing and letting die. There's a fine line between them when you withdraw life-support systems from a patient you are sure will die.

Moral obligation may be satisfied by more than one course of action.

ROGER: Well, I suppose there are some terminal situations where it would be better to kill than merely allow a slow, painful death.

DAVID: But that clearly misses my point. Whether you kill or allow to die, you are taking for granted knowledge of the

One cannot control the outcome of a decision.

29

situation that is not that clearly in your grasp. The determination of a rational, that is, moral, decision and of acting on that decision is within your grasp.

ROGER: Even if I were ready to concede to you the hazards of relying on the effects of the physical order, I'm certainly not ready to concede the certainty of the moral order. It's all very well to talk about how any rational person can derive a rule for action from your basic formula for moral law. It's quite another thing to be able to figure out what those rules of action are in the midst of a moral crisis.

Do people reason about rules in a moral crisis?

DAVID: You are quite right about that, but I don't think it tells against my approach. The formula I used to arrive at the rule that it is wrong to steal is universal and basic, but it is not necessarily how all people come by their moral rules. It is a justification formula, not a discovery or production formula. It tells us if the rules of action that we use are actually in accord with the moral law, but most of us don't learn those rules by applying that formula in a moral crisis. We learn those rules from our parents, our churches, our schools, from our acculturation into society. The rational formula can help us to critically evaluate that cultural orientation, but we usually find ourselves already equipped in times of crisis with rules we can apply.

The rational formula justifies moral rules, but people may learn these rules through acculturation.

GWEN: It is just that point I have problems with—knowing what is right. Even if we concede that the rule "stealing is wrong" or "you ought not to steal" were clear-cut and absolute, it may still not be so clear how to apply it in a situation.

DAVID: We need to clarify the starting points of principles and rules before we go to application. You and Roger have been pressing me for exceptions to rules in the face of hard cases. I have resisted that. I maintain that for a rule to be an effective rule in the moral order of things, it needs to be applied universally. I don't think we can make moral rules relative to particular situations for just the sort of reasons I've been arguing in the gunman example. This doesn't mean that moral rules are unqualified absolutes.

Universals must be distinguished from absolutes.

GWEN: I don't understand your distinction between universal and absolute.

DAVID: Moral rules can be qualified on the basis of principle and can still be universal in their application to any situation. As a matter of principle, it is wrong to kill or to do any act of

Moral rules can be qualified on the basis of a higher principle.

30

violence upon a rational being. Not doing violence is not only permissible; it's also a moral duty. Both of these rules are rationally derived from the higher principle that we must respect all rational beings as moral beings. Because it is sometimes necessary to use violence to prevent violence, as in the case of self-defense or war, we cannot prohibit violence without qualification. Our rule must be that it is permissible for human beings to use force upon other human beings to the extent necessary to protect rational beings from the violent acts of those other human beings. Sometimes that force will itself be a violent act, even killing the initial offender. So, the rule against violence must be qualified to provide for our duty to prevent violence. In this sense, it is not an absolute rule.

ROGER: It sounds to me like a rationalization for making rules relative to circumstances.

DAVID: No. Moral rules are universal just because they apply to all circumstances; they are not absolute, because they are qualified by reasons that follow from moral principles. The conditions are determined by reason, not by feelings in response to particular situations.

GWEN: Well, if I understand you, then your qualified rules make my problem about applying them even more difficult. If your moral rules and their qualifications are determined by principles of reason in the ways you maintain and are not relative to particular circumstances, how can you ever know which circumstances they are supposed to apply to? How can you know, given the qualifications, which conditions match up with which circumstances?

The problem is to match conditions with circumstances.

DAVID: There is a nice old logical formula for that. It's called a practical syllogism. The first premise is a universal principle or rule for action. The second is a characterization of a situation to which that principle or rule might apply. The conclusion is then the actual application of the rule to the situation. For your ship story, it would go something like this:

The practical syllogism is a formula for applying moral rules.

First premise: You ought not to steal.
Second premise: This [whatever the situation] is a case of stealing.
Conclusion: You ought not to do this.

GWEN: You have nicely exposed the character of my problem. It is discerning (in the second premise) that this is indeed a case of stealing. Your approach to morality not only allows for rationalization but it also invites it. Suppose my starving friend on the boat were to reason that taking food wouldn't really be stealing. If the owner of the boat were there, she would gladly give her some of the food to eat. If not as a beggar, then at least as a borrower it is all right for her to take some food. She can pay it back later. I find such rationalization quite reasonable. If it is a case of either begging or borrowing, it is not a case of stealing, and so your rule does not apply. This has some of the slippery-slope character you have already complained that my taking account of conditions would have. We all know that most embezzlers begin with the thought that they are really only borrowing from the company, not stealing, and genuinely intend to pay it back.

Does the practical syllogism invite one to rationalize situations?

DAVID: I must confess that my own problems with my approach lie more with doing the good than with knowing the good.

Another problem is conflict between knowing good and doing good.

GWEN: How do you mean?

DAVID: Often, my sense of duty is in conflict with my desires. It is one thing to know what is right; it is another to do it. I can know what is right but be so overwhelmed by my desires that I don't do it.

ROGER: I think our duties and our desires generally coincide, so that doing our duty also fulfills our desires.

DAVID: Then you may know you acted in accordance with duty, but your act may not have been motivated by duty. To act in accordance with duty by accident has no particular moral value, since it is not motivated by a good will. It is only when you act from duty, on account of duty, that your act is morally commendable.

Action in accordance with duty is morally commendable when it is motivated by duty, but not when it is accidental.

ROGER: So, I suppose you only act from duty when your desires are in conflict with your duty, in your view.

DAVID: No. Obviously, a benevolent person with warm concern for others may be just as morally motivated as someone who acts according to his duty in spite of an ill-tempered disposition or vicious desires. The point is that sometimes people act with morally wrong objectives—to harm someone, for instance—but quite by accident help him out instead. We don't find these actions morally commendable, even though we may be happy about the results. We don't usually *know* as clearly that

When duty and desire conflict, an act of will is needed.

our actions are morally motivated when our duties and desires coincide. It's easier to tell that we are morally motivated when our duty is in conflict with our desires. Then it takes an act of will to overcome desires in the service of duty.

ROGER: Just what is this act of the will supposed to consist of?

DAVID: It's a determination to act in a certain way or to keep from acting in a certain way.

GWEN: The determination to act in a certain way is already covered by your practical syllogism. Once you've got the conclusion, then that is what you do. That's what I was trying to state yesterday. To know the good is to do the good. A person naturally desires to do what she sees as good. She may say that she ought not do this, and then do it, but that's because she isn't really committed to the obligation. She may not have the rule well formulated, or may not see that it applies in this situation, or may have other aims or obligations that she takes as more important; but once she becomes convinced of what's right or best, then that's what she really ought to do and she'll do it.

Gwen maintains to know the good is to do the good.

ROGER: I have a somewhat different appraisal from Gwen's, though it may practically amount to the same thing. I suppose that all human action is motivated by desire or by habit. Since habits develop out of repeated fulfillment of desires, ultimately the only kind of conflict I find relevant is between one desire and another. If I am judicious about my actions, I may recognize that the fulfilling of a particular desire of the moment may in the long run prove undesirable. If so, my constraint on the immediate desire is not an act of will but merely attention to my desires of the long run, whether for fuller pleasure or for avoiding pain that would result from my immediate gratification. In none of this talk about desires, habits, and judgments is there any need for talk of the will, or even any place for it.

Roger contends that only a desire can effectively oppose desire.

DAVID: Maybe so, but neither your view nor Gwen's captures the awareness I have, and many people have, of an act of the will that follows decision and precedes action.

Neither captures David's sense of an act of will.

ROGER: If what you are talking about is psychological inhibition, that is a feature of human action that can be trained into dogs and other animals and has no particular moral sense. It simply brings to the fore what I take to be the most troublesome feature of your approach to morality; that is, its negative character.

Although your basic formula is set in positive terms, to always act so that you can will the rule for your action to be universal law, still, its effects turn out to be inevitably negative.

DAVID: I think that is so because rules generally set boundaries. To go back to our game analogy, rules constitute the limits within which the game is to be played. There may be strategies and tactics within the game for winning it, but they are not requirements for the game. The requirements for the game are only that you abide by the limits.

Rules set limits, and limits are negative.

ROGER: Just so! But the expectations of the game are that you win, succeed, fulfill some goal. If the only requirements for morality are that you stay within the limits, then morality has no positive direction and all it offers are inhibitions to action.

DAVID: And you propose as an alternative, I suppose, a basis of moral action in terms of desires and passionate drives.

ROGER: Well, desires at least give direction for action, but not all desires are good. Only those desires whose product is happiness can be considered good.

Roger claims good desires direct action to happiness.

DAVID: And how are we to know which actions produce happiness?

ROGER: On the basis of empirical evidence. Those actions that most contribute to happiness are the ones that maximize pleasure and minimize pain.

GWEN: Your understanding of empirical evidence is a little simpleminded. Desires may give drives to action, but they don't give direction. The direction is learned by the results of certain actions when desires are fulfilled repeatedly. We then commit ourselves to certain patterns of action as interpretations of those drives. People often have learned desires based on erroneous interpretations of their drives. They think that eating sugar gives them energy, where it actually takes energy away. They think tobacco calms their nerves, where it actually contributes to their nervousness. A more extreme example is people who eat to excess when they feel lonely because when they were younger their parents shoved food at them as a substitute for tender concern.

Desires may motivate actions, but actions are directed by the results of desires being repeatedly fulfilled.

ROGER: I don't think you are really arguing against me. What you are saying is that desires are not an empirical given but are to some extent learned. Part of moral education may very well be to learn to develop desires that contribute to happiness. The

Learning can develop the ends of desires as well as the means.

obese child who has mistaken hunger for love as a hunger for food has the pain of overweight as well as the pain of loneliness.

DAVID: I have other problems with your claim to an empirical basis for deciding on moral actions. One is that I don't see how it gets you from a description of the way people *do* operate to the standards for how they *ought* to operate. Another is how you are ever able to get from a concern for your own happiness to a concern for the happiness of others.

Can an empirical basis be adequate for morality?

ROGER: The two concerns you have are related, but the key to the relation is something I take to be basic to morality, which you have already rejected.

DAVID: What's that?

ROGER: The role of sympathy. We all have to a greater or lesser degree a sense of what another person's pleasure or pain feels like. I find myself saying "Ouch!" when I see a child fall and scrape his knee, and I even squirm with embarrassment over someone else's embarrassing situation. These feelings for other people bind my pleasure and pain to theirs. This involves me with their happiness as well as with my own.

Sympathy is one basis for morality.

DAVID: But as you yourself seem ready to admit, sympathy is not a reliable feeling, nor is it one that is equally distributed among human beings. When I am tired or preoccupied, I am not very sympathetic with the cares and needs of others. Does that absolve me of moral responsibility during those times? Some people appear never to be sympathetic, and others delight in the pain of others rather than in their pleasure. Does that mean we don't expect them to be moral?

ROGER: Not at all. I said that sympathy was basic, but I didn't mean to imply that it was all we needed. There is a practical principle that we can appeal to that doesn't rely upon how someone feels at any given moment.

DAVID: And what's that?

ROGER: Enlightened self-interest. You seem ready to concede that everyone naturally will seek his own self-interest to maximize pleasure and minimize pain. Otherwise, you wouldn't have voiced concerns about how we get to moral standards and social concerns. Once you take that step, you can see that if everyone pursues his own self-interest without restraint, then he will sooner or later bump into someone else's pursuit of self-interest. To ensure at

Enlightened self-interest is another.

least a moderate ability to pursue self-interest without conflict or destruction, everyone has to agree to laws that will guarantee that freedom to everyone. This is the conventional base for morality that I mentioned yesterday.

GWEN: But your two principles seem to pull in different directions, sympathy leading you to be concerned for other people's good, enlightened self-interest requiring you to avoid their harm.

ROGER: They pull in different directions, but they lead to the same place. If we had only enlightened self-interest, then my account of morality would be as negative as David's. I suppose that concern based on sympathy is the higher form of morality; but, as David points out, it's not something you can always rely upon. The two taken together give us a standard for moral action: to seek the greatest good for the greatest number, where good is to be understood as maximizing pleasure and minimizing pain. The principle of sympathy guides us to be concerned for the happiness of others as well as our own, and the principle of enlightened self-interest constrains us not to pursue our own self-interest to the point of damaging the interests of others.

The two principles together lead to the greatest happiness for the greatest number.

GWEN: I can see how this standard could get bent out of shape from the perspective of any particular observer. We're all prone to define and evaluate the interests of others in the light of our own interests.

ROGER: As a standard, we can ask how it would look from the perspective of an *ideal observer*, someone who had no vested interest in the issue at hand. Granted that no such observer exists, the idea of such a judgment can serve as a guide for deciding on the common good.

The standpoint of an "ideal observer" prevents distortion.

GWEN: I don't think so. It's not so clear that you can readily move from individual goods to common goods.

ROGER: I don't understand.

GWEN: You could start out with a number of light machine parts, but put together they make a heavy machine. You could take a lot of tasty foods and mix them together to get a very untasty combination. Whatever value things may have when taken separately or distributively—when taken one by one—they may not have the same value when taken collectively—when taken as a whole or in common.

ROGER: That distinction certainly holds for some things, but

I'm not sure I think there is any common good in that sense. We each individually can have happiness, but I don't think there is a common happiness. The best that we can have is the most happiness for the most individuals. There is no collective happiness.

"Common good," is the most happiness for the most individuals.

GWEN: That suggests you see no organic unity to any human community, not even the family, much less a religious or a political community. They are just tools to pursue individual, private desires.

ROGER: A more charitable appraisal is that communities are conventional structures where we can express sympathy and exploit self-interest and where we can seek the greatest happiness for the greatest number.

Communities are conventional structures to maximize happiness.

DAVID: I have a concern that is not quite the same as Gwen's but may point up the difficulty from a different angle. Your perspective opens the way to what is called the tyranny of the majority. What if we had a population that was two-thirds free and one-third slave. It would promote the greatest happiness for the greatest number for the slaves to serve the free so long as it made the free very happy, even though it made the slaves very unhappy.

Is there a problem of the "tyranny of the majority"?

ROGER: That assumes, of course, that the happiness of the two-thirds under these circumstances would exceed the happiness of all if all were free.

DAVID: Let me try a harder case. Imagine that it was possible to choose a world in which every person except one was in a state of everlasting bliss, but the price for that bliss is that one excepted person be in a state of everlasting torment. Could a moral person choose such a world?

Would the bliss of most justify the misery of one?

ROGER [after a pause]: I think not.

No . . .

DAVID: Then how can you maintain that your basic moral standard is the greatest happiness for the greatest number?

ROGER: Because a moral person would have sufficient sympathy for the person in torment that it would be impossible for him to enjoy the bliss himself.

but in such a situation moral people would not enjoy bliss.

DAVID: You take for granted that the person making the decision would not himself be the person in torment.

ROGER: I don't understand what you mean.

DAVID: Suppose you were the one to make the decision, but you were also the one to have the life of misery, with no hope of happiness. Could you, on your principle of sympathy, assume the perspective of an ideal observer and judge in favor of sacrificing your own happiness for the benefit of the greatest happiness for the greatest number? Would you even suppose that would be the moral thing to do?

ROGER: Even the most moral of men would have difficulty deciding for the greatest happiness for the greatest number under those circumstances.

DAVID: It seems that even without these hard cases it would be difficult for anyone to be moral in the sense you have described. You maintain that the ordinary man could not pursue my approach to morality because he lacked the power to derive the rules from my formula for the moral law. It seems even more obvious that he could not even manage to come to any conclusion about action from your approach. He would have to stop at every turn to calculate whether this action was the one that would contribute to the greatest happiness for the greatest number.

Could you ever calculate the greatest happiness for any particular act?

ROGER: If that were the way my approach worked, you would be close to being right. The moral man would have to decide for every action what is right or wrong. In fact, no one ever does that, and as a practical matter, no one could.

DAVID: How, then, do you avoid such implications?

ROGER: By recognizing that there are *types* of actions and situations. We don't need to decide for every single instance of action, since the significance of a given kind of action will be roughly the same from one situation to another.

One calculates on the basis of types of actions.

DAVID: In the end, that amounts to a recognition of moral rules.

ROGER: The difference, of course, is where we begin. Decisions on a kind of action for a kind of situation lead to habits on the part of individuals and to customs on the part of society. What distinguishes the natural order from the moral order in my account is the basis on which these habits and customs are established. They are morally based if they serve to foster the greatest happiness for the greatest number.

Decisions for moral acts are based on habits and customs that serve the greatest happiness principle.

DAVID: What you say now sounds a lot like what Gwen was saying yesterday about the motivation of people's actions.

38

ROGER: The difference is in the end. Once the moral principle has been used to determine the *type* of moral action for a *type* of situation, then that determination in effect becomes a rule to govern future moral action. It is such rules that by convention we write into law to promote the greatest happiness for the greatest number. This results in the moral principle ordering the direction that rules and laws will take over the long run, but it leaves individual actions in individual situations guided and limited by already formulated laws.

DAVID: So, practically, you combine your sensitivity for benevolence with an obligation to do your duty.

ROGER: Yes. It's very like a parent disciplining a child. He wants the child to maximize his happiness over the long run, but knows this is not best accomplished by meeting every immediate desire of the child. He also knows that he must take into account the needs and desires of other members of the household, and these are often in conflict with the immediate desires of this child. So the parent sets rules that will promote the greatest happiness for the greatest number. These rules may change over time as relations and conditions change, but they cannot be changed in the face of the demand of a particular desire. If they could, then we would in principle be thrown back to having to decide on every particular action and take the added risk of being guided by our immediate passions rather than by our moral principle.

GWEN: Now what you say begins to sound a lot like what David has been saying.

ROGER: But with some important differences.

GWEN: Such as?

ROGER: Well, for one thing, my understanding of rules allows for the kinds of conditional riders that you were suggesting earlier. I liked your employment of the analogy to natural law, and it seems much more appropriate to my understanding of how rules are formulated and evaluated. It makes rules interactive with the natural order rather than set apart in some absolute moral order. For another thing, my treatment allows for the change of rules over a period of time. This allows us to be flexible in determining what is right without sliding down the slippery slope that David exposed as a consequence of judgments of a particular situation.

These rules are relative to time and situation.

GWEN: It leaves you, however, with some of the same sort of problems we found with David's position. If David is worried about the tyranny of the majority in your hands, I'm worried about the tyranny of rules. Once you concede the priority of rules over needs and desires in the particular situation, you have overridden your moral principle on a case-by-case basis. Rules become more important in the specific instance than benevolence. In cases like my ship example, exceptions can be considered on your approach no more easily than they can on David's approach. It may be that you would eventually make conditions on your prohibitions against stealing, but only after a number of specific instances arise of this sort. Not only does that give no aid to the dying woman in my example but it also has conceptual problems of its own.

Does this lead to a "tyranny of rules"?

ROGER: Like what?

GWEN: Let's suppose one of your conditions is, Don't steal except when starving. That would prove too liberal for most senses of benevolence and would potentially give license to all sorts of abuses of the social order. As you start to specify your conditions further, you will be moving in the direction of a single rule for a single act. Although this gets you there by a very different route, it results in the same kind of problem that David presented me with when I suggested specifying conditions. A rule that applies to only one action in one situation is not much of a rule. By siding with David to avoid sliding down one side of your moral hill, you run the risk of sliding down another side, with the results at the bottom basically the same.

or to a slippery slope of specific conditions?

ROGER: It may be that in the end I am in a better position than either you or David to risk such slippery slopes. Because my moral principle can serve to correct rules, it can also serve to provide the best moral guidance over a period of time, even though the rules may require that some unspecified individuals suffer on occasion. This seems to me the best compromise one can draw between David's type of authoritarian ethic, on the one hand, and your apparently situational ethic, on the other.

GWEN: Mine is not a situational ethic, if by that you mean determining what is moral in the specific situation.

ROGER: Well, everything you have said so far has pointed to just that understanding.

GWEN: That's because everything I have said so far has been in reaction to what you and David have been saying. To set forth my perspective on these matters, I'd have to make a shift in focus.

DAVID: Before you do, I'd like to shift my bones a bit. How about a short break?

ROGER: Sounds good to me.

Coffee Break

ROGER: What did you mean, Gwen, when you spoke of "a shift in focus"?

GWEN: Well, David began with a focus on duty as the basis for morality, and that led to accenting the intention of the actor in evaluating an act. You turned to the worth of the activity in terms of what it achieves, and that led to a focus on effects. Intentions and effects are both aspects of the moral enterprise. Which you make your starting point and where you put your accent will determine your basis for moral decisions.

Is the basis of morality focused on intentions or on effects?

ROGER: And where do you put your focus?

GWEN: I am ready to acknowledge that both intent and effect are morally important, but I would put my focus on neither. Rather, I would start with a consideration of moral virtue. I think the more fundamental moral question is not so much what someone does as what she is.

Moral virtue is a third basis, focusing on who one is rather than on what one does.

DAVID: You talked yesterday in terms of goals and character and commitments. We might have thought your concerns with goals would lead to something like Roger's pursuit of happiness or that your focus on commitments would turn out something like a morality based on duty. It's not clear to me how attention to character is going to help us understand moral decision and action at all. You just are who you are. So what?

GWEN: That's true if you suppose that character is fixed. We do, however, talk of character development, molding someone's character, and change in character. We commend someone for having good character or reproach her for having bad character. If you want to talk of self-determination, how better than in terms of building one's own character?

One view is that character may change throughout one's life.

DAVID: I think of character mostly in terms of characteristics, of personality makeup. These matters are basically genetic and to some lesser extent products of early acculturation. I assume

Another view is that character is fixed at an early age.

that by the age of six years a person's personality is pretty well set, though some features of it may not show up until years later.

GWEN: That certainly sounds as deterministic as anything that either Roger or I had to say yesterday.

DAVID: And that's why I don't think of character as particularly relevant to morality. A person's character is what it is, and there's not much he can do about it. His moral commitments are not based on his character any more than they are based upon his feelings. They are based upon something he has control over, his will to abide by the moral law.

GWEN: My sense of commitment is somewhat different from yours and points up our difference in understanding the moral role of character. I see commitments and character as two sides of my personality. My character is who I have become as a person; my commitments are what I have projected myself to become. Viewed from one side, my character is my actual self, since it is what I have already become; my commitments are my potential self, since they are what I may yet become. Viewed from the other side, my commitments are my actual self, since they determine what it is that I actually do; my character is my potential self, since it determines the limits of what it is practically possible for me to accomplish.

Commitments and character are two sides of personality.

DAVID: That all sounds grand, but I'm not sure what it means or what relevance it has for the moral role of character.

GWEN: Well, practically what it means is that I can alter my character, within limits. Suppose that I tend, for a variety of reasons, to be tardy for appointments. Suppose that I become critically aware of how that reduces my efficiency, offends those I am to meet, and calls into question my virtue as a keeper of promises. So I commit myself to become prompt. This involves not only my promising to be here tomorrow at 8:00 A.M. but also my projecting a number of changes in my habits that will ensure my being able to make it on time. Such changes in habits don't come easy, and I might have to persist in attending to this project for months or even years until new habits are established.

Character can be altered by modifying habits.

DAVID: And what does all that you were going through a minute ago about actual and potential selves have to do with this?

GWEN: I have to start out with my character as an actual, given reality. If I don't think I'm prone to be tardy, or I don't think it's important to change, then I haven't come to terms with reality well enough to take up the project of becoming punctual. But I can also view my character in terms of its potential for change. If part of my character is a concern for efficiency, then I can use that to prod myself. If part of it is my urge to lie in bed each morning, then I need to take that into account as an inhibition to change and either calculate how to change that urge or recognize it as a limit to be dealt with. My project to become punctual is only potentially me, in that it is a characteristic I have yet to acquire; but even before it becomes a part of me, I have to carry it out in my actions. It is by actually performing that way that I eventually become that way.

DAVID: So where does the virtue lie? In *becoming* punctual or in *being* punctual?

GWEN: I suppose virtue is present in both cases. It's a little like the choice between your intent and Roger's effect. Both are morally relevant. We do indeed commend people for both effort and accomplishment. In most cases, however, the effort is seen as an instrumental good, as a means to an end.

Virtue lies in both becoming and being, in actual and potential character.

DAVID: Not every change is good, and not every effort is virtuous. What's going to count for good character and good commitments?

GWEN: The ultimate virtue seems to be integrity. Someone has integrity if he is able to integrate his character on the one hand and keep his commitments on the other. Often we have internal conflicts that you might characterize as conflicts between passions and a reasonable will or that Roger might characterize as between one desire and another. I think they more often stem from incoherent character or commitments. If one aspect of my personality doesn't integrate with the rest, then it will lead to the agony of internal conflict. My tendency to be tardy is at odds with my respect for other people, and if both are truly me, they are going to grind against each other in my everyday operations, rather than mesh to facilitate my actions. If I have political commitments that lead me where my professional commitments prohibit my going, then those spheres of my life won't always provide me with a good basis for integrating and orienting my life.

Integrity is the ultimate virtue.

DAVID: So you see the ultimate goal of your activity as integrating your character and your commitments?

GWEN: When you put it that way, it doesn't ring quite true.

I suppose that I see the ultimate goal of my activity as freedom of activity. That is true happiness, to always be able to act in accordance with your character toward the fulfillment of your commitments in an unimpeded fashion. Because we must continue to act in changing physical and social environments, that goal stands as an ideal that cannot be reached in practice, but it does serve as a goal that can be approximated and thus partially fulfilled.

The ultimate value is freedom of activity.

DAVID: That's a very exhilarating sense of integrity, but it seems to put an accent on ability and power without any significant moral constraints. The godfather of a house of the Mafioso would seem to qualify as virtuous under your characterization.

Is "the godfather" a man of virtue?

GWEN: Yes, in some ways, if he were a godfather of integrity. For that, he would have to be consistent in his judgment and character with the qualities that won him that position in the first place. He would also have to be coherent in his commitments and true to their fulfillment. In such a case, we might well admire him as a man of integrity. We could judge that he has virtue of a kind, even though he's a criminal.

Yes, in some ways . . .

DAVID: Then how can you maintain virtue is the basis for morality?

GWEN: Because the godfather's integrity is limited in scope and in coherence. It is limited to the community he governs and is seldom recognizable as integrity in the broader community. It's also likely to be flawed by ambition, viciousness, or other qualities that make it not hang together as well as it seems to. It is only apparent integrity.

but his integrity is limited in scope and coherence.

DAVID: This genuine integrity that leads to the freedom of unimpeded activity—how do you sort it out from the apparent integrity that is flawed by the limits of scope and lack of coherence?

How does one sort out apparent integrity from the genuine?

GWEN: What counts as integrity is closely tied to what it means to be human. What counts as best is the best human.

Integrity is tied to the meaning of "human."

ROGER: What counts as best is going to vary a lot from individual to individual. You and David and I seem to have very different concepts of what it means to be human. The differences are going to be greater from culture to culture. How are you going to avoid a cultural relativity of morality? You seemed to favor it yesterday but want to go beyond it today.

DAVID: To an extent there is a cultural relativity built into any notion of virtue. The Roman word for man was *vir*, from which our word "virtue" derives. The Greek word that we find translated as "virtue" can be more generally translated as "excellence in accordance with kind." For those cultures, the excellence for man—I'm not sure women were regarded as having virtue—was courage. The words "virile" and "virtue" come from the same Latin root, and we still talk of courage as being *manly* even today. If we see courage as maintaining integrity in the face of adversity, then we can see how close to the heart of things those ancients were. The move to a Christian culture was a move to charity as the prime virtue. God is love, and man was made in the image of God.

Is the notion of virtue defined differently in different cultures?

ROGER: So, Gwen, how do you choose between a Greek and a Christian conception?

GWEN: Your very question already indicates our ability to give critiques of cultures. To a certain extent we are bound by our own cultural perspective, which includes Greek courage and Christian charity, but we may now be more dominated by affluent acquisitiveness. However, just as we can talk of the actual, potential, and ideal characteristics of individuals, we can consider cultures in the same terms: what they actually are, what they practically can become, and what they ideally ought to become. The ideal is set by the fullest development of human potential through unimpeded activity.

We can critique culture on basis of human ideals.

ROGER: You seem to be arguing in circles about how we can become what we ought to become and how we ought to become what we can become. When you shift from individuals to cultures, you do just what you accused me of doing with the relation of individuals to societies. You suppose that your characterization of individuals applies to the culture as a whole.

DAVID: Worse than that. You set up a conception of morality that only the most able and the most powerful can relate to. Common people don't even aspire to, much less participate in, such a self-realization ethic. Your morality is only for the power elite. The best that the rest can hope for is to follow the rules laid down by the more powerful. That strikes me as a less noble source of moral law than the moral law based on reason that I proposed.

How can an elitist morality apply to everyone?

GWEN: I can't agree. The best for the rest may well be example following rather than rule following. If indeed the culture recognized the virtuous man, the person of integrity, the woman of character, as the best sort of person to be, then people will seek

Morality is acquired through example.

to be like that person. This is true discipline, because it is acting like a disciple, following the leadership of one who teaches through example. Children are more likely to follow the examples their parents set than to follow the rules their parents lay down. In the same way, people will follow the examples of those who are best.

ROGER: But without rules, you have no social guarantee of concern for other people. All your talk of virtue and self-realization seems very self-centered to me.

Is the self-realization focus self-centered?

GWEN: It is self-centered, but that simply goes back to the need for an adequate conception of the self. I understand persons as fundamentally social. Without a society in which I can relate to other human beings, I am not fully a human being. These relations with other people not only serve as sources for my character and objects of my commitment but also they are integral to what counts as being me. To be self-centered in the usual, narrow sense is to be less than oneself and to undercut one's own integrity.

Yes, but the concept of self must include relations with others.

ROGER: Not everyone has your sensitivities for conceiving self so broadly. I still think your way leads to a self-seeking self-centeredness that is socially debilitating in ways that my sense of self-interest is not.

GWEN: I think the *fascism* and the *egoism* that David and you believe characterize my approach are both real dangers, but they are dangers that can be avoided. The difficulty I have with my own conception is more basic, and I don't see how to avoid it.

ROGER: What's that?

GWEN: Whatever the practical difficulties with self-determination as becoming your commitments, there is a fundamental conceptual difficulty. To become what I project as my new self, I must deny a part of my old self. I think that extreme forms of this are similar to what Christians mean when they talk about conversion. Self-realization becomes self-denial. I must give up the old self to get the new self, but it has to be the old self that does the giving up. What is more morally pertinent, to achieve a new level of integrity, I must break old commitments, which is a denial of integrity. This is not just giving up an old integrity for a new one but also a denial of the foundation stone of integrity, that one keep her commitments. Somehow, I don't think a wife divorcing her husband is justified by telling him that he is no

Is self-denial the price of self-fulfillment?

longer integral to her life. Still, to maintain any sense of current integrity, she may have to deny commitments she had previously projected for her current self. I see no way out of this kind of compromise of integrity. We are just better promise-making animals than we are promise-keeping animals.

ROGER: Wait a minute! Maybe this problem, along with some of your other difficulties, comes from your not really going far enough in thinking through your approach. You have talked a lot about character and commitments, virtue, integrity, and freedom, but you've said very little about goals. All the things you talk about seem more like tools to enable you to pursue goals, rather than ends in themselves. I suspect that underlying it all, you have a notion of happiness as the ultimate aim, a notion very similar to mine.

Character and commitments, integrity, and the like seem to be means rather than ends; the end may be happiness.

GWEN: I'm not sure how much my understanding of happiness fits in as an ultimate aim, but I am sure that it is a very different conception from yours.

ROGER: You need to explain yourself.

GWEN: When you speak of happiness, you treat it as pleasure or the absence of pain. I suppose that pleasure is not a meaningful goal of action and that pleasure and pain are not opposites.

Happiness is not pleasure; pleasure is not a meaningful goal of action.

ROGER: Come on! I can see your maintaining that pleasure is not a moral goal, but it is obviously a meaningful one. Just look at all the pleasure seekers in the world and you'll see plenty of evidence that it's not only meaningful but also operational.

GWEN: Pleasure is something that happens to you; it's not something that you do. You, Roger, would say that it's the result of action, but I don't think it's the result of action in the way that something is the product of skill, like making an artifact, or even in the way that something is the effect of a cause. You may say that doing certain things or having certain things give you pleasure, and you may even think that it is because of the pleasure that you like the doings and havings. I think it is because you like the doings and havings that you find them pleasurable. I also think that your pleasure is more variable than your likings. Sometimes you like things even when you don't find them particularly pleasant.

DAVID: And pleasures are more unreliable, too. This is where Gwen's notion of commitments makes some sense to me. Most people talk about love as a feeling, but feelings are what happens to you, not what you do. If love is a feeling, then it comes and goes, and it isn't in your control. That's not the sort of love you can will or even be obligated to do. If you treat love as a commitment to a kind of relation, then you can act on that commitment. That makes sense of Jesus's command. There's no way to understand pleasure as other than something you feel. So it's not open to will or obligation.

ROGER: I didn't suppose that it was. I've never proposed pleasure as something you do; only as something you seek. I like your treatment of love, but it is quite compatible with my conception of pleasure. A love relation is one in which I seek the pleasure of the other as well as my own. I can see that as a commitment going beyond judgments of self-interest or even beyond feelings of sympathy. But it is still in pursuit of pleasure. In fact, it is easier to see pursuit of pleasure in my concern for someone else in a situation where I'm explicitly giving pleasure or relieving pain. Didn't you ever give someone a backrub? What did you think you were doing if not giving pleasure and relieving pain?

Roger counters that the pursuit of pleasure is a goal that may include commitment and concern for others.

GWEN: Yes, I've given a lot of backrubs, and I suppose that when I give one, I am doing a lot of things for which pleasure and pain are incidental. Pain is a symptom of something out of order in a person's life. Alleviating pain is putting that order right. When I give a backrub, I break down knots in muscle fibers, and that relieves tension, reduces nervousness, and generates a sense of harmony and well-being. All of this usually gives pleasure, but that pleasure is not the object of my doing what I am doing. It is a by-product of the activity and serves as a sign that I am successful in getting the results that I wanted. When I give backrubs, I'm also getting into physical contact with another person in such a way that it will reliably improve my relations with that person. That, too, will give us both pleasure, but it is the relation, not the pleasure, that I seek. The pleasure is again a by-product of and a sign for the improved relation.

Pleasure is a by-product of action.

ROGER: I find all this unconvincing support for your claims. You say that pleasure is a by-product of the good results of actions, a sign that you have been successful. If it is a reliable sign— whenever you get good results, you get pleasure, and whenever you get pleasure, you know you have good results—then why do you want to distinguish the sign from the object? If you don't think it is a reliable sign, how can you be sure that your results are good? You also clearly treat pleasure and pain as opposites in your talk about backrubs, whatever you want to claim about them abstractly.

GWEN: I guess I think that pleasure as the absence of pain is too simpleminded a notion. Some pleasures are just relief from pain, but that would make pleasure a negative notion, and the logical end of a morality based upon a pleasure principle would be contentment as the absence of activity. We seem to have a very different logic for the notion of pain from that of pleasure. We locate pain physically in ways that we don't locate pleasure. You may have a pain in your left leg, but pleasure is a state of being of the whole organism. Pleasure is not even a sensation on the same scale as pain; although certain sensations may *give* pleasure, we never speak of sensations as giving pain—the sensations are themselves painful. Although we recognize kinds and degrees of both pleasure and pain, we don't always correlate the more pleasurable with the less painful. You do recognize one pleasure as more or less pleasurable than another, don't you? *Pleasure and pain are not opposites.*

ROGER: Of course. Pleasures can be more or less intense, more or less enduring, more or less free from painful side effects.

GWEN: Are you willing to acknowledge that pleasures differ in kind? Are the pleasures of listening to music or reading a book comparable to taking a shower, winning a court case, or making love? *Do pleasures differ in kind?*

ROGER: They're all different in kind as I experience them, but I'm not sure it wouldn't be possible to reduce the qualitative differences to quantitative ones.

GWEN: How about good and bad pleasures? Are some pleasures better than others? *Are there good and bad pleasures?*

ROGER: Yes, certainly. But bad pleasures have to do with painful side effects in the long run, not with anything about the pleasure. No pleasure is bad in itself. Whether some pleasures are in themselves better than others is going to depend mainly upon whether we can reduce the qualitative differences to quantitative ones.

GWEN: Well, you still seem convinced that it makes sense to pursue pleasures, but do you also think it makes sense to ask whether a particular pleasure is good?

ROGER: Yes, of course, it does.

GWEN: If that is so, then you can't be taking pleasure as your ultimate principle to determine what is good. *Can pleasure be an ultimate principle if there are good and bad pleasures?*

ROGER: Oh, yes I can! I've already shown how. I can compare

pleasures with other pleasures, or I can trace the consequences of getting the pleasure to see if it leads to lessening pleasure or increasing pain somewhere farther down the line. You have yet to show how your conception of happiness is different from my own.

GWEN: Well, I suppose that happiness is a sense of power growing. It's not contentment, and it's not the absence of pain. Growth is almost invariably painful, but it's a happy sort of pain. I don't want to say happiness is the ultimate end of the moral endeavor, since my understanding of happiness is in *becoming* virtuous. *Being* virtuous is as important as *becoming* virtuous, and the exercise of virtue is often a focus of our moral concerns.

Happiness is sense of power growing.

DAVID: You don't want to say happiness is a *sense* of power growing either, since that makes it something you feel, rather than something you are or do; and it makes your view subject to the same criticism you leveled at Roger's view.

GWEN: You are right about that. The difference is between being happy and knowing you are happy. If I focus on my feeling of growth, that's like Roger's focus on pleasure. It is a *sign* of the value, not the value itself. The value is to become more fully human.

Better: It is becoming more fully human.

ROGER: I don't want to say that we have to stop for today, but we do. The session has lasted longer than we planned, and we've certainly raised more issues than we've answered. We need to get on with the question of whether all of these differences in approach to the problems are going to make any practical differences in the results of our deliberations over specific cases. I suggest that we meet in the conference room tomorrow at 9:00 A.M. to finish up our preliminary explorations.

GWEN: But David and I still haven't explored the differences between his duties to rules and my obligations to persons.

DAVID: I think we can both see where that would lead us. We share your sense of obligations to persons, but you don't see obligations as backed up by unconditional rules. But Roger is right. We have to quit sometime. Maybe you can give us a quick summary of where we have been today, Roger.

ROGER: Into a lot of argument and controversy, obviously. But we are beginning to see a structure. Gwen's suggestions about our differences in focus were good ones. That you focus on intentions, she on character and commitments, and I on results makes good sense of some of our differences and may in the long run point to ways that are not so incompatible. It may be like the blind men touching different parts of the elephant. David, your talk of moral law is something we can all relate to, but in very different ways. You see it as similar to the formal laws of mathematics, required by the conceptions you deal with and the logical inferences you draw from them. Gwen treats moral law as more like physical law, required by the natural makeup of human beings and subject to error of formulation and application in ways similar to natural law. I see moral law as more like civil law, dictated by the purposes of the community that formulates it and determined according to convention.

Is moral law similar to the formal laws of mathematics, physical law, or civil law?

GWEN: You tend to blur differences, Roger, just so you can get on with things. You've interpreted our positions in terms of law. That biases the whole discussion in your favor, to put it mildly. Other than that, your summary doesn't say much more than what David said yesterday. I'm beginning to despair of seeing any relation among our positions that will make working together possible.

ROGER: Well, I see two ways to relate our positions, and I'm the man in the middle on both. David and I have some agreement about the role of rules in moral decisions, and rules seem to have little or no importance in Gwen's approach. Gwen and I both see some importance to happiness as a goal of moral action, even if we differ in our senses of happiness. Happiness seems to have no comparable value for David. I am as pleased as I am surprised to come out as a sort of bridge between the two of you, but I find myself wishing that you had a comparable point of contact.

The role of rules and the goal of happiness are differences in approach.

DAVID: I think we probably do. It's just in an important area that we haven't yet explored—the same tangent Gwen noted we left dangling yesterday. We still haven't talked about the relation of moral matters to religious and legal ones. I think it's somewhat ironic, Roger, that whereas you and I are closer in explicit religious commitments, Gwen and I are closer in our understandings of what they mean. I think this is important stuff, but I have to agree that the schedule doesn't allow for it. I have a suggestion, if you think your wife will hold still for it.

ROGER: What's that?

DAVID: That the two of you come over to my house for supper tonight. I think my son and his wife will excuse me from my date with them. If you can leave your wife in the lurch and Gwen can get free from the hospital for a couple of hours, we can chew on some of these matters after a good meal.

GWEN: I had hoped we could limit these preliminary explorations to one more meeting, but as you say, it was my idea to talk about those other issues. Maybe an evening away from the hospital will help take some of the tension out of our differences. I'm working this afternoon, but I'm not on call tonight. Would you like to come over to my place?

DAVID: We began today's session with a compromise over my sexism, although I noticed that you lapsed into talking about *man* at one point yourself. Let's not rearrange the evening on the basis of sexism. I assure you that I am not only a competent, but an excellent, cook. How about it, Roger?

ROGER: I guess that I can go along, especially if you are as good a cook as you claim.

DAVID: Fine. I'll see you both at seven.

Questions for Reflection & Discussion

1. Roger has trouble understanding David's sense of moral law. Do you? How is it different from physical law? How is it different from the rules of a game?

2. Roger draws a distinction between what is permitted and what is required. Why does David think this misses the point of the application of the moral law to theft?

3. Gwen introduces the story about starving on the boat. David calls it a slippery-slope problem. If you start allowing conditions on morality, there is no stopping place. Do you think Gwen or David is right about this problem? Why?

4. David said you can be sure about moral judgment, but not about practical results. On what does he base that claim? Do you think he's right?

5. How does David distinguish universal rules from absolute rules? Can he make sense of qualified rules without making them relative to situations?

6. David introduces a practical syllogism for applying rules to situations, but then has a disagreement with Gwen about the relation of knowing the good and doing the good. What position do you take on that disagreement, and why?

7. Roger introduces sympathy and enlightened self-interest as prin-

ciples for moral decisions. Is that a change from the position he took in the first meeting? If so, are the two positions compatible?

8. Roger introduces the notion of the "ideal observer." Could such an observer even be thought of without the prejudices of one's own perspectives?

9. Roger moves from maximum happiness for the individual as a goal to the greatest happiness for the greatest number as a goal. What is Gwen's objection? Do you think she is right?

10. David gives Roger a "hard case" for his maximum-happiness goal. How would you answer David's question? Do you find Roger's answer consistent with his principles?

11. How does Roger attempt to reconcile the goal of happiness with his notion of the role for moral rules? Do you think the pursuit of happiness based on rules would be better than happiness pursued on the basis of individual actions?

12. Gwen maintains that Roger's treatment of rules leads to a slippery slope of its own. Do you think she is right? If so, is there any reliable way to avoid this problem?

13. David and Gwen disagree on whether a person can change his character. Do you find Gwen's account of character change plausible?

14. Why does Gwen reject the godfather as an example of a person with integrity? Do you find her argument convincing?

15. Gwen maintains that children are more likely to follow examples than rules. Do you think she is right? Why?

16. David calls Gwen's position elitist and Roger calls it self-centered. Is either right? Why?

17. Gwen poses a problem for her own position that implies a compromise of integrity. Does this undercut her whole moral orientation? Why?

18. How do Roger and Gwen differ in their understandings of the role of pleasure in moral action? Who do you think has the more accurate understanding?

The Third Meeting

THE SCENE IS at the dinner table in David's home after dinner the same evening.

GWEN: This is a very nice liqueur, David. What is it?

DAVID: It's Grand Marnier, a mixture of cognac with an orange liqueur. It doesn't appeal to everyone's taste, but it's my favorite.

GWEN: I'm a little surprised that you regard drinking alcoholic beverages as a matter of taste at all.

Is drinking a moral issue?

DAVID: What do you mean?

GWEN: I guess I assumed that you would oppose drinking categorically, on both moral and religious grounds.

DAVID: You apparently still don't quite grasp how my moral approach gets applied to specific actions. I don't believe I can generalize about drinking in an unqualified way, one way or the other. I can generalize about taking care of one's body: One should never act in such a way that it will cause basic, irreparable destruction to his body. Then, from that law it follows that if I am an alcoholic, I shouldn't drink. This is clearly conditional, because it is the application of a general law to more specific conditions, but the general law itself is not conditional.

One view appeals to the qualification of rules.

GWEN: Specifying the degree of destruction to your body

sounds conditional to me. It at least offers an opportunity for rationalization, which, as I complained earlier today, is one of my difficulties with your whole approach. Still, my appraisal of the drinking issue winds up not far from where yours does. I suppose that it's not so much a matter of whether you drink, but how you drink. The standard of moderation will vary from individual to individual, depending on how they are physiologically, psychologically, and socially affected. One meaning of being alcoholic is to drink compulsively to excess. This not only makes the drinking activity not free but it also debilitates other powers of operation. That comes under the classification of self-destruction in some important sense. But what about your religious limitations?

Another, to moderation of action.

DAVID: Even old puritanical Paul recommends a little wine for the stomach, and there's one place in the Bible that suggests Jesus liked eating and drinking enough for some to call him a glutton and a drunkard. I don't find much ground in the Bible for teetotalers. I think abstinence has come from the realization in an individual's life that he can't handle the stuff. He then falsely generalizes that understanding to everyone. Just because he is logically able to will that everyone abstain, it doesn't follow that everyone should. A lot of generalizations that are logically possible are not morally necessary. What *is* morally necessary is that you not act unless you are able to will the rule of your action to be a universal law.

ROGER: Well, I can see that a good dinner hasn't taken away your appetite for argument. For my part, I see drinking as a moral problem where it presents threats to the well-being of other people, but not where it threatens the individual drinker.

A third states that the drinking issue is not morally relevant on an individual level.

DAVID: I would expect, given your greatest-happiness principle, that you would be concerned for his happiness too.

ROGER: Indeed I am, but it is beyond my responsibilities, and even beyond my prerogatives, to impose my sense of happiness upon another individual. The law should guarantee that his drinking, or any other behavior, not bring harmful effects to other people. That's why we legally limit his privileges by excluding driving when drunk; forbidding public, disorderly conduct; prohibiting the beating of his wife and children; and a number of other abuses of others. When drinking leads to such bad effects, it is clearly wrong. But if someone chooses to drink himself to death, that's his business, so long as his doing it doesn't prevent others from pursuing their own happiness.

Laws are to protect us from harm by others . . .

DAVID: Surely, you don't mean for us to take you literally. That's the same as morally approving suicide.

ROGER: There have been times when people have come to the conclusion that they would be better off dead, and so would the world around them. If it seems fairly clear that their killing themselves does not bring harm to others, I see no reason to prevent them from pursuing it. It seems patronizing for me to tell them that I don't think they are really maximizing pleasure and minimizing pain. Also, I don't think suicide is anything you can legislate against, since you can't really punish someone who kills himself.

but not to protect us from ourselves.

GWEN: As you know, people do legislate against drinking. There are some states that have "dry" counties.

ROGER: I think those are bad laws—bad because they invade people's privacy and bad because they attempt to legislate morality.

GWEN: I thought you were in favor of legislating morality and that you regarded drinking as a matter of taste so long as its effects don't harm others.

ROGER: We seem pretty much in practical agreement among ourselves about the drinking question, even though we understand the foundations for the conclusion in very different ways. But we all know there are others who see drinking as an evil or as a sin. For them, it is a basic moral question, and I am offended by their imposing their moral sensitivities on me. Even if I agreed that drinking were a moral issue, I would regard it as wrong to impose that morality on others.

It is wrong to legislate morality.

GWEN: Well, either I've misunderstood you or you seem to be arguing out of both sides of your mouth at once.

ROGER: What do you mean?

GWEN: When we began, you maintained that morality talk was just a way for people to express their approval or disapproval of an issue or to persuade others to adopt a certain attitude. Later, you unfolded a moral theory for us in which you exposed as a basic principle the greatest happiness for the greatest number. Is the sense of "morality" the same in both cases? Are you giving us a kind of persuasive definition of morality to get us to accept your principle?

Isn't the greatest-happiness principle inconsistent with the idea of morality as persuasion?

ROGER: Perhaps. I don't think I'm inconsistent in my talk

about morality, but I may not always make clear how I'm talking about it. When I talk about legislating morality, I'm talking about those people who approve or disapprove of something and then attempt to impose their feelings on others by enacting laws that support them. This ceases to be persuasion and becomes coercion. Talk about morality in this context describes what people do and do not approve of. The moral principle of the greatest happiness for the greatest number is not a principle to determine morality, but rather a principle of utility, a way of managing the maximization of morality. It does not tell people what they should or should not approve of, but given a description of that, it tells people that the most rational way to maximize what they are after is in terms of social utility. This is not legislating morality; it is a matter of good management.

GWEN: I'm not sure you can effectively make such a neat distinction between your analysis of other people's morality as expressing feeling and your proposal that moral principle is just a matter of prescription for good management. But your way of putting all this points up a more pressing problem for me. You slip very easily from the moral to the social to the legal. You seem sometimes to talk about them as though they were equivalent in meaning, and at other times you talk as though they are distinct concerns. Your shifts seem to be at your convenience. When David suggested just now that suicide was morally wrong, you came back with the remark that suicide was something you couldn't legislate against. This suggests understanding morality in terms of legality. When I responded with a remark about legislating against drinking, you called that bad law. This suggests legality is something different from morality. At the same time, you maintain that morality is a social concern, and yet it isn't clear to me that you can equate social expectations with either moral ones or legal ones.

ROGER: Again, I think I've been consistent, but maybe not so clear. Let me see if I can distinguish among these concerns. An individual has a moral code insofar as there are things he approves and disapproves of, things he praises and blames. If this expresses nothing more than his individual concerns, then it means no more than a claim for his own preferences and perhaps an invitation to share them. So far, no moral requirements have been made. If, however, he expects agreement and cooperation, then there has to be some social basis for that expectation. Either he needs some special status (as a boss or as a father, for instance) or there has to be some social understanding of how things ought to be done. These social understandings don't need to be in the form of laws. They can be established customs for the ways things are to be done. It is only when society needs to enforce its expectations that it needs law, and then it needs sanctions, punishments, for breaking the law. Blaming someone for suicide doesn't make sense, since there are no social or legal sanctions you can impose on a dead person. Prohibition of strong drink by law is an attempt to make personal preferences a matter of social understanding by imposing legal sanctions. It's just this sort of shift by the prohibitionist from personal preference to social expectation to legal sanctions that amounts to legislating morality.

GWEN: Then how do you justify the idea of legislating the greatest happiness for the greatest number?

ROGER: Legislation has basically a limiting function. What I said earlier today about David's rules applies equally well to legislation. Laws ought to protect people's rights to pursue their happiness. Where such pursuits are competitive, then the laws ought to seek regulation that will on balance provide the greatest happiness for the greatest number. But I don't suppose that laws ought to require morality of people *except* to ensure the rights of others.

Laws ensure rights.

GWEN: I'm beginning to see what David had in mind this morning about our differences with you. I see moral issues bound to social issues because man is basically a social animal. In my view, then, social morality is an extension of individual morality. You seem to think there is a sense in which there is no individual morality, since everyone naturally pursues his own desire for happiness. Your understanding of society doesn't seem to be organic with what it means to be human at all. Society seems to be a kind of moral convenience necessitated by the fact that we occasionally bump into one another in our individual pursuits of pleasure. The legal then becomes a regulation by society of those individual actions that threaten to encroach on the rights of others.

For Gwen, social morality seems an extension of individual morality; society is an organic whole.

ROGER: You treat my view of society a little too crassly. You must remember that I began my account this morning with two principles. You have taken account of only one. In addition to enlightened self-interest, there is also sympathy. But you are right insofar as you see that I don't take society as a given of the human condition. Unlike you, I suppose that someone can be

Roger sees society as a human construction, not a given of the human condition.

58

quite human without society. Society is something you construct, both as a fulfillment of the sense of sympathy and as an expedient for enlightened self-interest. Although David surely would disagree in his reasons for it, I would expect him to take a somewhat similar view. I find nothing in his notion of a moral law that points toward a view like yours.

DAVID: There you are wrong. Gwen sees man as basically a social animal; I see man as basically a rational animal. But I suppose that man's rationality implies his social nature. Since this social nature is a logical requirement, rather than a practical construction, I see myself as closer to Gwen than to you on this point. You were maintaining earlier today that my understanding of the moral law was basically negative. It is just in such social implications of rationality that it is not. If all humans are lawgivers as moral agents, then this lays a basis for a community in their common rationality and common morality. This implies we should never treat other human beings simply as means to our own ends. They deserve the same respect that we accord to ourselves as rational lawgivers. Insofar as we are able to realize in practice this mutual respect in pursuit of the moral law, we are approximating the ideal of a kingdom of ends in which all of our goals are in accordance with the moral law and all of our actions are respectful of other persons. So, the moral law implies that we always treat others as of worth in themselves, not merely as means to our ends, and that we always act to bring the ideal kingdom into fuller reality.

David contends society is a logical requirement of a rational nature.

ROGER: I can see how, on that basis, you would not only agree with Gwen that the social is a part of human nature but also agree that there are private dimensions to morality as well.

GWEN: I'm beginning to get confused over the use of words like "private" and "individual." It seems to me that "private" is not in contrast to "social" but in contrast to "public." Some people tend to equate the personal with the private and with the individual. Then they suppose that if a matter is personal, it is not anybody else's business. Something like sexual intercourse is usually private, hopefully personal—in David's sense of regard for the sex partner as a person and in my sense of involving an integrating human relation—but it is never individual. It is social so long as it involves the society of two individuals. I would go so far as to say that it *ought* to be personal, and I know it often is not. I suppose that much of sexual engagement is self-seeking

The opposite of "private" is "public," not "social."

in the narrow sense, having no regard for the other as a person and involving no enrichment of a personal bond. From what you have said so far, Roger, I suspect you would not regard these as moral issues.

ROGER: Your division of terms is clarifying and helpful. I think you are right in pairing individual–social, private–public, personal–impersonal. Maybe what I want to say is that private matters are not moral matters—but that won't quite work either. I can imagine business deals that would be morally reprehensible just because they were never made public. No, I think the dividing line for me is between the individual and the social. If it is a matter of strictly individual concern, then it is not a moral matter. I'm not sure, Gwen, that you recognize any matter as strictly individual.

Another contrast is between "individual" and "social."

GWEN: In a certain sense, that is so. Obviously, my experiences are my own, and in that sense different from your experiences. To that extent we are individual. But even you acknowledge "feeling with" other people, and I want to add to that a dimension of judgment as well. When I commented on David's Grand Marnier earlier, I was not simply expressing my feelings about it. I was making some judgment of its worth. It makes sense for me to say that it is good, even if I don't particularly like it. In this way, I suppose that matters of taste are disputable.

Are matters of individual taste matters of dispute?

ROGER: I do not.

GWEN: And that points to our disagreement about individual morality. I suppose that I can make the judgment that excessive drinking is bad for other individuals. This is a moral matter because it has to do with the person's well-being in the senses I outlined earlier today. It is as morally relevant for persons who drink in private as for those who drink in public. Since it is a judgment about the activity instead of an expression of my preferences, it makes sense for me to say to another person that she ought not to drink to excess, and it would be an expression of concern rather than an invasion of privacy for me to tell her so.

Are matters of individual well-being moral matters?

ROGER: I'd think you were butting in where you didn't belong.

DAVID: What about the issue of sexual relations? Do you find private sex as well as private drinking to be beyond the scope of moral scrutiny?

ROGER: We need to keep in mind Gwen's distinctions among private, public, and social. Because sexual intercourse is a social act, it at least has the potential for moral relevance. Because it is also ordinarily private, it is not readily subjected to *sanctions*, to any kind of legal or other social restraints. I don't share your conviction, Gwen, that it *ought* to be personal. Each partner can treat the other as an object and through a symbiotic relation gain pleasure without inflicting pain, finding enjoyment without any sense of personal tie to the partner. I suppose if there is some grievance on the part of one of the partners, he would have to appeal to the sympathy of the other to keep things private and make things right. Otherwise, he would in some way have to make things public—show the results of sadistic abuse, for instance—to gain any social redress. Ordinarily, anything goes sexually between consenting adults. A lot of jokes are made about the match between a sadist and a masochist, but I suppose there are a lot of such matches in real life, and I see nothing morally wrong with them.

In sexual relations, does anything go?

GWEN: You are getting legal sanctions mixed with moral obligations again.

DAVID: Worse. Your treatment seems to imply no restraint on any activity or on any relation in sex.

ROGER: Yes, premarital and extramarital sex as well as marital; homosexual as well as heterosexual; group sex as well as couples; experimental sex as well as coitus. The *only* constraint is the mutual consent of the adults so engaged.

The only constraint is mutual consent.

GWEN: In your approach to things, there doesn't seem to be any reason to make an exception of children. Why not just let "consenting" cover everyone? David might argue with this from the standpoint that children have not arrived at the age of reason, and I might argue that they had not yet developed the ability to make judicious decisions. I find no comparable ground for your making them an exception.

ROGER: Well, there are limits to my aversion to paternalism. Children need parental guidance until they come of age in some sense.

DAVID: I'm far more concerned about your liberality than about your limitations. Do you mean to draw no distinction between marital sex and extramarital sex?

ROGER: I understand the marriage relation to be a social

contract. The obligations to society at large have mostly to do with economic stability and child rearing. The terms of the relation between the couple are matters to be worked out between them. Many of the marital conflicts that I have become aware of in divorce suits stem from the couples' never having made explicit their expectations in the marriage relation. Now people tend more and more to write down these expectations in the form of an explicit contract. Some couples expect exclusive sexual intimacies as a part of their contract; others do not. Where this is expected and explicit, then extramarital sex is a violation of the contract and thus is immoral. Where there is no such expectation or where the contract is not explicit, then there is no immorality in extramarital sex. The immorality is not in the sex act but in the violation of the covenant.

Marriage is a contract in which agreements about sex need honoring.

DAVID: Please excuse me for being picky about words again, but you just shifted from "contract" to "covenant." It may be that in your vocabulary they convey roughly the same meaning, but in mine they do not.

ROGER: Just what sort of contrast did you want to draw?

DAVID: Contracts are like business deals. You make promises, and you get promises back; you have obligations to fulfill your promises and expectations that the other person will fulfill his. In a convenant, a person invests more of himself than the time, money, or effort that may be required by a contract. A covenant is something you enter into and become a part of.

ROGER: Sounds a little biblical to me.

DAVID: Perhaps it does, but let's just keep to marriage for the time being. If I have a marriage *contract*, then I've made a deal to keep some promises and get some benefits; and if I break my promises or fail to get my benefits, then the contract has been broken and that's grounds for divorce. If I have a marriage *covenant*, then I enter into a personal relation with mutual understandings, a relation that will grow and develop and may even alter the understandings with which it began. The covenant takes on an organic unity over and above the individuals who have entered into it. There is no longer just him and me—there is us. Because that unity exists, breakdowns in understanding, even violations of trust, do not automatically give a basis for dissolving the covenant.

A contract is an agreement about promises and benefits; a covenant is a personal relation that develops over time.

GWEN: You are beginning to sound like me, David, talking

about organic unity in relations of individuals. I like your notion of covenant, even though it is biblical. It nicely expresses how I feel about human relations as realities that involve something of what the related individuals are. It's just for those reasons that I don't suppose Roger could ever accept your distinctions between contracts and covenants.

ROGER: You're right. The two notions are roughly the same in my vocabulary. I think what you describe in terms of an organic unity is indeed no more than a complex of contracted promises and benefits. I don't suppose that the terms of the contract are unalterable over time, nor do I suppose that a single infraction would necessarily nullify the contract. Our difference in understanding the relation is that I don't see anything in the relation that is more than the people who are doing the relating. I don't think your conception of an organic unity adds anything to the relation, either.

Roger contends contracts and covenants are equivalent.

DAVID: Perhaps I can suggest an added dimension. God in the beginning ordained marriage as the relation between a man and a woman in which they become united. Marriage is a creation of God in the natural order. It's what he ordains as the natural state for the preservation of the human race and for the well-being of man.

David maintains marriage is a relation ordained by God.

GWEN: And woman, too, I hope.

DAVID [politely ignoring her]: This ordination of marriage by God makes it more than your legal contract, Roger, or even than an organic covenant. It makes it a part of nature, sanctified by God's own design for man.

GWEN [breaking in, again]: You are starting to confuse moral, natural, and divine laws, like Roger does moral, social, and legal issues.

What is the relation of moral, natural, and divine laws?

ROGER: We really do have a new dimension of your moral philosophy, David, that is not included in your formula for moral laws, unless I miss my guess. In addition to what is ordained by reason, you now want to tack on what is ordained by God. Surely you are not going to claim that what is ordained by God can also be derived from what is ordained by the formula you gave us this morning, that we should always act so that the rule for our action could be made a universal law.

DAVID: I rather suppose what is ordained by God is consistent with what is ordained by reason, but I also suppose there is a dimension of revelation in God's ordinances and that they are not directly derivable from reason. God gives us a general revelation in the natural order of things. Through understanding the natural order of things we can come to understand better the moral order. To this extent I have some sympathy with Gwen's approach. He also gives us special revelations through his saving acts in history, like the exodus of the Hebrews from Egypt and the ministry, death, and resurrection of Jesus Christ.

God's ordinances are consistent with reason but also come from revelation.

ROGER: I am as ready to proclaim my devotion to the Christian faith as you are, but I have a very different slant on its moral significance. I suppose God's revelation in Jesus Christ dictates *that* we should be moral, but it does not reveal in any particular way *how* we should be moral. I have never been able to discover anything in a religious ethic that gives any kind of special directives that are not already contained in a nonreligious one. The laws of Moses look very like the code of Hammurabi, and the golden rule of Jesus is different only in detail from a similar rule laid down by Confucius.

GWEN: And if revealed morality does make a difference, what then? How can you be sure, David, that it will not conflict with reason?

DAVID: Because God is good, and a good will implies a will governed by reason. The medieval thinkers debated whether God's will or his reason is more basic to his nature. If we begin with God's goodness, we can see that it binds his will and his reason into one, and that dissolves the problem. Because God is good, his will always operates within the bounds of reason. This is what lays the basis for the moral order as well as the natural order. God's law governs both, and man's law is made in the image of God's law, just as man is made in the image of God.

God's law is rational and moral.

GWEN: I feel uncomfortable about your appeals to God in much the same ways that I feel uncomfortable about your appeals to rules. We've all heard some version of the argument, "God exists, because the Bible tells me so, and I know whatever the Bible tells me is true, because it is the will of God." Such arguments as these presuppose the commitments they are arguing for. In the same way, appeals to rules don't make sense unless you are already committed to the rules. To base the rules on commitments to reason and revelation just pushes the conditions back one step. I don't suppose even these commitments are without qualification.

Appeals to God, as well as appeals to rules, presuppose the commitments they are arguing for.

DAVID: Perhaps the only thing I can do is to point to the reality that is given and say, "SEE!" Rationality is basic to getting along in the world. If you want to say that is a practical condition, all right. There may be problems with God's special revelation but surely not with his general revelation. The natural order is a manifestation of God's natural law.

GWEN: I haven't expressed my reservations very well. I suppose that we are each born into a cultural frame and that our maturation and acculturation consists of taking on habits and commitments that integrate us with that culture. Our religious commitments are a part of that acculturation process. Most children adopt the religious frame of their parents or at least of some broader community. Radical departures from such a framework are called conversions. Some of us convert out of the religious community rather than into it.

Is religion an aspect of culture?

DAVID: Your sociological account so far seems pretty innocuous. What is your point?

GWEN: My point is that appeals to reason and natural law are only going to have effect within a community commitment.

DAVID: When the community of commitment is broad enough to include virtually the whole human race, then that doesn't seem very problematic. The rationality of the moral law and the revelation of the natural law transcend the boundaries of particular cultures and religions.

GWEN: I suspect they are not nearly as universal as you suppose them to be. I don't want to labor the point. I'm more interested in pursuing my earlier concerns with conflict. Suppose someone has committed herself to certain obligations in her family life, in her vocation, and in her job, and there are conflicts with her religious devotion. Then she must choose among them.

Religion is one sphere of commitment among many, and there may be conflict among them.

DAVID: Your spheres of obligations makes good sense as a way of describing a way of life, but your characterization of the religious sphere doesn't satisfy me. In one sense, the religious is a sphere of operation in a worshipping community. In that sense, it is a sphere of obligation coordinate with—and sometimes in conflict with—other spheres. In another sense, the religious is devotion to God. As such, it includes all spheres of life and lays a basis for reconciling conflicts between them.

David sees religion as a base for reconciling conflicts.

ROGER: However you and Gwen place the role of religion in moral decision making, David, I think you share with her the

65

difficulty she mentioned this morning about her own approach, and you don't have even her way out of the bind.

DAVID: What bind is this?

ROGER: Whether or not your revealed morality places demands on you that are inconsistent with your rational morality, it seems inevitable that at least some people in some practical situations will have conflicting duties. Someone may have the duty to be faithful to his wife, loyal to his country, not to lie, and not to kill. He may get into a bind when, to maintain loyalty to both wife and country, he must either lie or kill. Gwen would rationalize her way out by reevaluating her commitments. You don't seem to have such an option.

Roger contends conflicts are inevitable, in spite of religious morality.

DAVID: I would suppose that such a bind lies not in the incompatability of rules but rather in their application to the specific situation. You haven't really generated a situation where it is clear that the rules for action *require* their incompatability in application. You have merely supposed there are such situations. If indeed I were confronted with such a situation, I would throw myself upon God's mercy and "sin boldly," as Luther put it. [Pause] Let's leave the dishes and finish our coffee by the fire in the living room.

Coffee Break

GWEN [later, by the fire]: Why do you suppose that conflict of commitment is a difficulty that David and I have that you escape?

ROGER: Because you begin with a multiplicity of principles in your commitments and spheres of obligation. David begins with a single formula, but it generates a plurality of unconditional rules. I begin with a single principle, to maximize happiness, and that admits of no rivals.

A single principle is needed to resolve conflict.

GWEN: You actually began with two operating principles, sympathy and enlightened self-interest.

ROGER: And again I must tell you that they are only means to implementing the greatest-happiness principle.

GWEN: I still think from that principle you generate rules

66

that put you into the same sort of bind you project for David. *Can appeals to*
But all this is beside the point I've been trying to get to on the *principle always resolve*
religion and morals issue. Let me try with an example of a specific *conflicts among law,*
case. A small girl is brought to the emergency room of the *religion, and morality?*
hospital. She has been hit by a car and is suffering from internal
hemorrhaging. She requires an operation to save her life. While
I am preparing to perform the operation, her parents appear on
the scene. They tell me that it is all right for me to patch her
up but not all right to perform surgery. Cutting into the body
is a procedure prohibited by the divine revelation of God and so
is against their religion.

DAVID: They are simply wrong about God's revelation.

GWEN: Their error may be simple, but its correction may be
virtually impossible. They may say to me just as you did a few
minutes ago, "SEE!" And if I fail to see, they will say that God
has not revealed the truth to me. The practicalities in this case
are that the law requires me to get their permission before I
operate on their child. That's their right as parents, but my duty
as a doctor is to save their child's life if I can. So we have family
duties and religious duties and professional duties and legal duties
working at odds in various ways. What, under these
circumstances, should I do?

ROGER: Here's where an element of virtue does come to the *Is it ever right to break*
fore. Is it ever right to break a bad law? Well, ideally, the law *a bad law?*
ought to be brought into line with the greatest happiness
principle, but that can only be in the long run and usually after
challenge. The law must be respected, and yet it is in conflict
with morality. The only moral answer seems to be to break the
law openly, to declare the moral grounds on which you break the
law, and to take the consequences in the punishment that society
measures out. That would take not only moral discernment but
also a lot of courage.

DAVID: A law that is in conflict with moral dictates is not a *A law that is in*
bad law. It is in reality no law at all. Our civil law gets its *conflict with morality*
sanction from natural law, which is derived from divine law. God *is no law.*
has given us reason both to formulate and to apply moral law.
When a civil law is formulated that is contrary to the moral,
natural, divine order of things, then it can't be regarded as really
law.

ROGER: So, would you advocate that we disregard such
apparent laws?

DAVID: No! Just because it has the appearance of a law, it needs to be followed, out of respect for the very notion of law. Otherwise, we invite a disrespect for law that will encourage people to abide by the laws they like and violate the ones they don't.

But even apparent laws must be followed out of respect for the idea of law.

ROGER: So, you would have to let the child die. Again, we have the old sin-of-omission-is-better-than-sin-of-commission routine. The effects of not operating are the same as killing the child.

DAVID: It is a sad conclusion but the only moral one I can figure out. Even an apparent law commands respect because it is in the form of a law.

GWEN: All this talk about apparent and real law doesn't make much sense in practice. The only laws there are are real laws. Laws are human artifacts that contribute to the constitution of the state much as commitments contribute to the character of the individual. We can fairly well predict future development of laws and their interpretations by observing the constitution of a state and the situations with which it interacts both internally and externally. Altering laws in the state is like altering commitments in the individual. It comes about as a result of a crisis of integrity. In such a crisis, there is always a sacrifice of an aspect of integrity as a means to attain a fuller integrity. The measure of integrity in the state is the degree of freedom for fulfillment of potential that it can guarantee to its individual citizens. In a period of change, some will suffer to effect a reconstitution for the welfare of the whole. In my example, it's a choice among the parents, the child, and me. Something's got to give. I just have a strong sense that it shouldn't be the child.

Laws express the constitution of the state and are only one factor in conflict.

ROGER: You both seem to work so hard to link law to morality. In an enlightened state with able legislation, there will always be efforts to maximize happiness, whether motivated by sympathy or by enlightened self-interest. But the reality of law lies neither in the ordinances of God nor in the constitution of the state. It lies in convention backed by the power to command. There would be no law were it not legislated by men and backed by the enforcement of sanctions and punishments.

Laws are conventions made real by sanctions.

GWEN: But what about rights? Surely this child has a right to live, a right that outweighs her parents' rights to pursue their religious practices.

What about rights?

ROGER: The child has no rights other than those given him by the state. In my view, duties are established by laws, and rights are correlated with duties. It is the command of the law that creates duties and also sanctions for failure to follow duties. These sanctions are the only guarantee we have for rights, since they protect people by enforcing the duties. The rights don't even come into being without the duties and the sanctions. Although moral human beings ought to be guided by the greatest-happiness principle, that moral guide gives no guarantee for rights. Rights, like duties, are matters of convention established by law. There are no human rights except those that are acknowledged by law.

Roger maintains rights are conventions established by laws.

GWEN: It seems more accurate to say there are no rights except those that are established by the constitution of society. Social consciousness often gets ahead of legal commitment. It seems to be our understanding that people have rights that lead to their enactment into law, not the other way around. Without that understanding, they can't be said to have rights; but with that understanding, society lends a kind of moral force that functions in a similar fashion to Roger's notions of legal sanctions to guarantee rights.

Gwen says rights are established by the constitution of society, which in turn creates laws.

DAVID: Your account shifts the focus from the legal to the social, but the concept seems basically the same as Roger's. For him, rights change with majority vote; for you, they change with the drift of social attitude; for both of you, they seem to be no more than a conventional acknowledgment of the status quo, with no critical basis for directing the change. Roger winds up with a kind of moral schizophrenia, with moral direction outside of the realm of the law and with moral rules only within the realm of the law; and there is no guarantee he can get them together. You, Gwen, seem left with a kind of cultural relativism: What is is what ought to be.

GWEN: Your criticism would be just if we were not measuring our understanding against the constitution of reality. Having rejected your real–apparent distinction regarding laws, I have to introduce a similar one regarding rights. What you might want to call real rights, I would want to call potential rights. Our understanding of children as persons is different from that of Roman times, for instance, and, on the whole, better. We thus accord rights to children that the Romans didn't. You would say children *really* had the rights then, even though the Romans didn't acknowledge them. I would say they had them *potentially*

Rights are potential because they exist in our constitution as human beings, but our actual rights are what society accords.

then, because it was their nature to have the rights, but their society was not actually according the rights to them. They couldn't *actually* have the rights until they were guaranteed the exercise of those rights in society, and that guarantee had to wait on social understanding. So the only *actual* rights we have are those our society *understands* to be our rights, but the potential rights are there in our constitution as human beings.

DAVID: I'm not sure you got my distinction between real and apparent law straight, but I think that if you press your treatment of actual and potential rights, you'll find yourself on the way to a conception of natural rights. You want to say rights are constituted by nature; I want to say they are ordained by God; in either view they are *there*, they are real, independent of what people think of them. It's our duty to discover, acknowledge, and abide by them.

David thinks potential rights imply a base in natural rights.

ROGER: Do you suppose that the child on Gwen's operating table has a right to life when life can be preserved?

DAVID: I certainly do.

ROGER: Then I think I have your test case I was looking for earlier. You want to maintain a duty to follow statutory law, and you want to maintain a duty to defend natural rights, and you have a case here where they are in conflict.

There may be conflict between natural law and statutory law.

GWEN: Whether David manages to resolve his conflict or not, we seem to have pretty well fleshed out our views on social, legal, and religious matters as they relate to moral concerns. What we said at the outset about marriage seems to serve as a summary of what we maintain about social and legal issues generally. What I suppose is constituted in individuals as commitments and between individuals as social covenants is constituted in the state as laws. Laws, like social covenants and individual commitments, arise out of an existing constitution and point toward the development of a projected constitution. In each case—individual, social, and legal—integrity and freedom remain central to moral concern. Roger begins with no moral concerns at the level of individual interest. Moral concerns in his account only arise out of a conflict of interest and so are not generated until such conflicts arise at the social level. There the conflict is resolved by a contract, which is a product of convention containing promises and implying obligations. What law seems to add over and above this contract, in your account, Roger, is the power of sanctions, the organized social force to guarantee that the promises of contracts

Recap: One position is that moral concerns arise out of conflict at the social level and are resolved by contracts, or laws.

70

are kept or at least that penalties will be exacted or redress will be made if they are not. On top of this, law guarantees the general welfare in such areas as criminal law, but only with the same conventional resolution of conflict into duties and sanctions that you already described on this level of social contract.

ROGER: That seems about right. The rationale for the law is in terms of the social contract, but the power for fulfilling the social contract lies in the sanctions of the law. So, the social is conceptually prior to the legal, but the legal is practically prior to the social.

GWEN: David maintains a position on the other side of me in terms of natural law. Where I would characterize the individual, the social, and the legal in terms of organic unities whose integrities are constituted by commitments, you find in each, David, a rational order founded in nature and ordained and sanctioned by God. This is why you come out for natural rights, while I maintain rights can only be actualized in a society that acknowledges them, and Roger maintains the only reality that rights have follows from the duties and sanctions derived from the conventions of statutory law.

Another perspective sees moral concerns in terms of organic unity between the individual and society, and a third in terms of ordination and sanction by God.

DAVID: You have adequately stated the perspectives and rightly placed yourself in the middle between Roger and myself. I think yours is an unstable position that must sooner or later fall off the fence, if not in the direction of my naturalism, then in the direction of Roger's conventionalism.

ROGER: I think all three positions find a common denominator in my treatment of contract.

GWEN: That is only because you persist in ignoring the conceptual differences among your notion of contract, my notion of covenant, and David's notion of ordinance. Your contracts are nothing more than the actual words they are written in. My sense of convenant expresses the constitution of social relations, and David's notion of ordinance lays claim to disclosure of the will of God in the natural order.

Parallel distinctions lie in the notions of contract, covenant, and ordinance.

ROGER: Whether these conceptual differences imply significant practical differences is the task we have assigned for ourselves for tomorrow morning. I'm ready to call it a night. I have come to appreciate David's claim that you two do have something to share. What you share seems to be the other side of the coin from the challenge he put to me about my greatest-happiness principle.

Remember? He asked if a moral man could will the happiness of all except one person at the price of that person's agony. I have a similar problem for the two of you. Let's put you into a lifeboat together—since I suppose you'll wind up in the same boat anyway. Let's put a number of other people into the boat, and for personal interest, give them characters. One is a young mother carrying her infant child; another is an old, withered woman in her eighties; there's a criminal who was being extradited to face justice, but whose captor went down with the ship; there's a middle-aged couple who are rather nondescript and who seem to have nothing much to recommend them except their love for each other; there's a frivolous rich heiress and her gigolo; there's an immigrant on his way to join his family whom he hasn't seen in years; there's a vagrant stowaway and a beautiful movie star. All these people are in the boat with you, and you are too many for the boat's capacity. If you all stay, it's a certainty that the boat will be swamped and you all will drown. Who gets thrown overboard, and how will you decide?

In the lifeboat, who gets thrown overboard?

DAVID: No one gets thrown overboard.

ROGER: Exactly the response I expected. I don't even suppose you could morally justify jumping overboard yourself. The practical upshot is that your moral position requires that you all drown. At least my moral position would lead to the practical result that most would be saved.

GWEN: I'm not sure I'm forced into the same boat with David, though you may be right. It will give me something to think about before I fall asleep. Let me give you a story for your bedtime. You probably know the story of *The Lord of the Rings*, which revolves around a ring of power that makes the wearer of it invisible.

ROGER: Yes, it's one of my favorite stories.

GWEN: Well, I think it is based, in that part at least, on an ancient Greek story about a shepherd named Gyges. Gyges discovers his ring while tending his flock and, when with a group of his shepherd friends, figures out that it makes him invisible. He then in short order puts on the ring, seduces the queen, kills the king, and takes over the kingdom. Without the constraints of social sanctions, any sense of morality that he had vanished. I don't suppose that would be true for David or for myself. I do suppose it would be true for you, if you are true to the moral orientation you have expressed. Your orientation seems to imply

Does morality vanish when you put on Gyges' ring?

that your sense of morality would vanish when you put on the ring.

ROGER: Whether that's true or not, it's a fun bedtime story. I will enjoy dreaming about what I would do with Gyges' ring. Thank you, David, for having us over, and thank you, Gwen, for the bedtime story.

GWEN: I hope your dreams are not too perverse. Goodnight Roger Shepherd. Goodnight to you, David, and many thanks, not only for the meal, but also for making the discussion possible.

DAVID: Goodnight to you both, and thanks for coming. See you in the morning.

Questions for Reflection & Discussion

1. Does Roger find suicide morally justified? On what basis? Where do you stand on this issue and why?

2. Why is Roger against "legislating morality"? Do you agree?

3. How does Gwen distinguish individual–social from private–public and personal–impersonal? On this basis, why does Roger maintain moral issues are always social?

4. Under what conditions does Roger regard sexual relations and actions to be morally relevant? Under what conditions do you? What does this imply about the similarities and differences of Roger's moral orientation to your own?

5. Does the distinction that David makes between contracts and covenants make sense to you? Does it require reference to God and the Bible? Why?

6. How do Roger and David differ on the relation of morality and religion?

7. Why does David suppose that the revelations of God will not conflict with the requirements of reason? Do you find this convincing?

8. How does David meet the challenge of the problems of conflicting commitments and duties?

9. Is it ever right to break a bad law? How do David, Roger, and Gwen answer this question? How do you answer it?

10. How does Roger's treatment of rights by legal convention differ from Gwen's treatment in terms of social constitution?

11. How does Gwen's treatment of potential natural rights differ from David's conception of actual natural rights?

12. Do you suppose there are natural rights? Name a few, if you do. Is your view of their basis more like Gwen's or more like David's? If you don't suppose there are natural rights, then do you agree with Roger or do you have some alternate view?

13. Whom would you decide to throw off Roger's lifeboat? On what do you base such a decision?

14. What would you do if you had Gyges' ring? What does that imply about your understanding of the relation of moral decisions to social and legal sanctions?

The Fourth Meeting

THE SCENE IS a conference room at the hospital the next morning.

ROGER: Well, we're down to our last meeting on the foundations of moral decision. After this, we'll have to go on to consider specific cases and policies. The task for today is to determine whether our differences in theoretical orientation imply significant differences in practical application. Do either of you have any need to recap what has gone before, or do you have any suggestions about how to proceed on today's topic?

GWEN: I have a little of both. I don't know what you dreamed about Gyges' ring last night, but you had me lying awake for hours with the lifeboat problem. In thinking through what I would favor doing in that situation, I got a clearer focus on some of the differences among us and also on some of the problems each of us faces because of our respective approaches to ethics. I think we have clarified sufficiently what our approaches are, but I would like to summarize a few points on methods and problems, if that's okay.

ROGER: Go ahead.

GWEN: You may remember that your criticism of my approach, Roger, included a charge of potential narcissism, that concern for virtue might lead to such a preoccupation with oneself that she might fail to have any concern for other people. David's criticism was almost the opposite. He saw the hazard of a person getting so caught up in the ethics of a power elite and in concern for the integrity of the broader community that she might well lapse into fascism. I saw the one problem as a deviation from the norm in one direction—failure to recognize the basically social nature of human beings—and the other as a deviation from the norm in another direction—failure to maintain a critical perspective on one's own society. They amount to perversions of the approach rather than the results of the approach. The problem that I myself presented was basic to the approach itself. It amounts to a kind of crisis of commitment, in which to be true to yourself you have to engage in denial of yourself.

Personal integrity approach has the potential for narcissism or for fascism, and it confronts a crisis of commitment.

ROGER: Yes, I see all of that.

GWEN: Well, I also began to think of our criticisms of you, and they seemed to fall into a similar pattern. Even before you had presented sympathy as a basis for your greatest-happiness principle, David was arguing that decisions qualified by sympathy are not reliable bases for morality. He was arguing against my presentation of situational conditions in the starvation story, maintaining that it was a logically slippery slope down to the level of a rule for a single situation. It was you, Roger, who came back with the claim that the relativity of situation need not be that specific, nor the contingency of the situation so unreliable, that we need to abandon conditions in favor of the absolute. Later, when I claimed that specifying conditions under which the rule would apply gives the same logical effect as proliferation of exceptions to the rule, I used the image of sliding down one side of the hill with one problem and down the other side with the other. In short, it was deviation from the norm in one direction or in another. Your retort was that your principle gave a basis for critical revision of the rules, saving you from slipping into deviation. Still, the problem that David confronted you with in terms of the tyranny of the majority seems basic to your approach and doesn't come from a deviation from your norms. I want to call it a crisis of exclusion, because it requires you, in order to preserve the well-being of some, to deny the well-being of others.

Greatest happiness approach may lead to proliferating exceptions on the one hand, or a tryanny of the majority on the other.

ROGER: You may remember it was that same difficulty that I claimed as a virtue in the lifeboat example.

GWEN: Exactly why I want to call it a crisis. You found the problem a definite moral handicap when David confronted you with it initially, but in an actual crisis situation you were able to embrace exclusion as the only way out of the problem that was in tune with your approach! Exclusion is inconsistent with your principle of sympathy, but required by your principle of self-interest—no, even that isn't adequate; it's required by the principles of sympathy itself. To fulfill sympathy to some, in some situations you have to deny sympathy to others. The best you can do is to maximize happiness, just as the best I can do is to maximize integrity.

Exclusion is inconsistent with the principle of sympathy, but required by it.

DAVID: I would begin to feel a little left out of this discussion if I didn't suspect that you were about to fabricate a similar problem pattern for my approach.

GWEN: I don't have to fabricate it. The pattern is already there, even though our criticisms of you only touched upon it obliquely. Don't you remember Roger characterizing your position as authoritarian and his showing impatience with any suggestion that passivity is preferable to activity, that sins of omission are better than sins of commission? Well, those seem to me to be your two directions deviating from the norm. To be arbitrarily rigid in maintaining a rule in the face of the needs of a situation is an authoritarianism that is a deviation from your principle of a good will, not an expression of it. You argued against that deviation by developing conditional rules to relate the absolute rules to actual situations. I suspect that the passivity problem is also a deviation from your norm, but I don't think you argued against it, and that's why you went down with the lifeboat last night.

The problems with the rationality approach are that it may tend to be authoritarian on the one hand and tend to be passive on the other.

DAVID: I hope you are not going to maintain that I am caught in a dilemma between authoritarianism and passivity, where my avoiding the one problem throws me into the other.

GWEN: No. I don't suppose they are logically tied together in that way. I do suppose that your approach leads to a conceptual crisis that is similar in its role to the ones I described for Roger's and for mine. The crisis for your approach would come when you had two absolute rules that implied contradictory actions in a single situation, where you would have to lie to avoid stealing or steal to avoid lying, for instance. You maintained that your practical applications through intermediate conditional rules could avoid that trap, and we never came up with a clear counterexample. Still, you admitted in principle that such a situation would be a crisis for your approach and that you would

The crisis for the rationality approach occurs when two absolute rules imply contradictory actions in a single situation.

have to "sin boldly" to meet the crisis. I take that to mean you would have to act contrary to the good will to fulfill the objectives of the good will, and the result in your case, as in Roger's or mine, would be to make the best of a bad situation according to the guide of your approach to morality.

ROGER [going to the chalkboard at the end of the room]: We can outline what you have been talking about along the lines of an excessive accent on individual values on the one hand and on social obligations on the other. It would look something like this:

	Individual	Social
DAVID	Inactivity	Authoritarian legalism
GWEN	Narcissism	Fascism

David would confront a crisis of evil, an inability to do anything good, by avoiding errors on both sides. But I don't quite see how your crisis of commitment comes into the scheme of things. I also don't understand your attempt to construct a similar scheme for problems with my position.

GWEN: I think you are doing one of your lawyer's trips on us again. You want to set up the conditions to make it look like you win and David and I lose. Just to play your game, let me see if I can fit what I said before about your approach into your model. If you continue to proliferate exceptions to the rule long enough, which is to deny group or social values in favor of individual ones, you run the risk of an individual relativity, where the judgment depends only on the individual. If you continue to call attention to conditions of a social and physical sort, you move in the direction of a contextual relativism, where judgments depend completely on the situation.

ROGER: That sounds like a set of problems for your position as much as for mine. Besides, you haven't made it very clear just how proliferating exclusions is practically different from proliferating conditions. And on top of that, I don't see any relation of all of this to a crisis of exclusion, in which the tyranny of the majority is supposed to exclude the minority.

GWEN [going to the board]: Well, maybe my scheme isn't perfect, but it looks something like this:

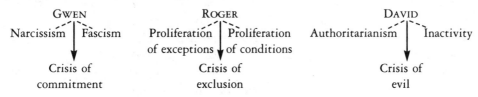

The broken lines show ways of getting off the moral track that each of us set for ourselves. They are deviations from the norm. The individual–social divide may have something to do with it, but I don't think that's all there is to it. The solid lines show a direction that is a problem arising from sticking to the norm of each position. The crisis comes when the moral position taken at least appears to demand conflicting things.

DAVID: I think what you have outlined for Roger as deviations from his position is actually the more basic crisis problem of his position. Because he takes empirical conditions into account the ways he does, either by exceptions or by qualifying conditions, he's going to come out with an equation of the practical with the moral in the end. That amounts to saying it's right because it works for me, which makes a mockery of morality.

ROGER [ignoring David's last charge]: I don't think David is yet ready to admit that what you call his crisis of evil would ever arise in an actual situation. That would basically undercut his norm of rationality.

DAVID: Quite the contrary. I would continue to deny that such conflicts were in *principle* irresolvable for just the reason you mentioned. I do think there are a lot of actual situations where, given the limited time and the limited ability of the decision maker, the only options a person can figure out may well be a choice between two evils. I am ready to embrace the reality of the crisis of evil just because of our limited and fallible nature. I think the diagram gives a neat layout of the problems for each of our positions, but I still don't see how it relates to your solution to the lifeboat problem, Gwen, or how it is going to help us in our efforts as a committee.

How does the latter diagram help with the lifeboat problem or with other problems?

GWEN: Just because the lifeboat problem was a crisis-of-commitment situation for me all over again, I didn't want to sink in the lifeboat with you, David, but I didn't want to join Roger in throwing someone overboard either. It seemed at first to me like a genuine dilemma, where I was damned if I did and damned if I didn't. Then, somehow, reflecting on the patterns of problems we each had made me realize that I was buying into the problems of your approaches rather than trying to deal with the problems in terms of my own approach. I was seeing my options in terms of your options and not being true to myself.

DAVID: And what did you come up with for your option?

GWEN: Consensus. Which is different from majority rule and also different from unanimity. With majority rule, we'd wind up throwing someone overboard. If we waited for unanimity, we'd all go down with the boat. For consensus, we need to have a mutual understanding that it is the sense of the group that a certain decision is the best thing to do. This may require some individuals to go along with the sense of the group, even though their individual judgment may favor a different plan of action. What is required is a willingness on everyone's part to do it this way, even though not everyone may want to do it this way. In the case of the lifeboat problem, no one would get thrown off against her will, but it's not likely that everyone would go down together, either. A problem with answering the question in the abstract is that I don't know what the specific answer would be apart from the actual group in the actual situation.

It may lead to consensus based on mutual understanding.

DAVID: That begins to sound a bit like the situational ethic stuff again.

GWEN: There's an obvious sense in which every ethic is a situation ethic, since the decision has to be made in the particular situation, but there is an equally obvious sense in which a lot of the deciding work is done ahead of time. One of the effects of rules, commitments, habits, and the like is to eliminate options. If we were open to all of the possible options at the time of decision making, we would not be able to resolve the problem in time to be practically effective. On the other hand, we don't want to eliminate options in such a way that we are unable to respond to the needs of the particular situation. It's like finding the friction point between the clutch and the accelerator on a standard shift car: too much clutch and the car won't go; too much accelerator and you will kill the motor.

In one sense, all ethics are situation ethics, but a lot of the decision making is done ahead of time, according to rules, commitments, and the like.

ROGER: It's just such pressures for a practical resolution to a moral problem that sometimes forces us into a majority vote. We can't always wait for a consensus. It's often something that can't be forced in a crisis situation.

Some situations require majority vote.

DAVID: I'm not sure I would ever find a majority vote a satisfactory resolution to a moral problem. A vote gives no guarantee that something is right. If it did, that would justify every case of mob rule.

Does majority vote justify mob rule?

GWEN: The methodological disagreement that we have over the lifeboat case seems likely to continue with us in our committee work. To extend my analogy, we each have different friction points for getting started. David uses a lot of clutch and very little gas and doesn't get started very fast, if at all. I use as little clutch as possible, and try to gauge my gas to get off to a smooth start. Roger uses a lot of clutch and a lot of gas and gets off to a fast, sure start, even though it's often jerky and uncomfortable.

ROGER: After hacking through your imagery, I gather you're telling us that our differences in method of group decision is largely a matter of style and degree.

GWEN: Not at all. David made clear he closes out on majority vote; that's clearly not a matter of degree. You may prefer consensus in the luxury of unhurried deliberation and I might accede to a majority vote in the dire extremity of impending doom, but the difference is not merely a matter of style.

The difference between consensus and majority is more than stylistic.

ROGER: Well, for the purposes of this committee, the difference has to be a practical difference to count, and that is the matter we have yet to explore.

DAVID: It seems to me that we have already tentatively explored the difference between consensus and majority in a number of our problem illustrations in earlier sessions. Your lifeboat example, Gwen's starvation-on-the-ship example, my pursuit-by-the-murderer example all served as examples for application of our moral principles, and each one found us basically disagreeing in one way or another. They're all made-up examples, but they can be translated into real problems of moral conflict pretty readily.

Examples so far have been test cases for moral decision.

ROGER: Let's try a type of hospital-related problem, just to test you out.

DAVID: All right. How about abortion? It seems fairly evident that you, Roger, are going to come out with a permissive outlook, particularly since the law asserts the right of the expectant mother to her own body and you maintain no other rights than statutory rights. I favor absolute prohibition of abortion on the grounds that it amounts to taking a human life, and that's murder. I also want to maintain that the unborn infant has rights that are his by virtue of being a human being. I would expect Gwen to be an indecisive in-between or else appraise the issue on a case-by-case basis.

Abortion is considered as a new test case.

ROGER: The whole question of the rights of the unborn is a part of the broader question of the rights of future generations, and it doesn't admit of simple answers even if the sense of rights

81

is limited to just those rights guaranteed by law. I suspect you are right about my appraisal anyway, especially if you limit abortion to the first two trimesters of pregnancy. Until the fetus is viable, it counts as a portion of the mother's body, or even as a parasite living off a host, if you like. As such, the mother's needs and prerogatives take precedence over any that may be imputed to the fetus. The portion of your characterization that I don't find acceptable is your own position. If I projected a situation in which aborting the fetus would save the mother's life but kill the fetus, you might still hold out against abortion on your omission-is-better-than-commission thesis. If the situation is one in which both mother and fetus will surely die without an abortion—where the cervix will not allow passage of the head and it is too late for a cesarean, for instance—then omission of action implies that both will die, and action requires that one or the other life be sacrificed. Is it so clear in this situation that you would avoid action or favor the child over the mother?

A situation may arise where inaction sacrifices both mother and fetus, and action sacrifices one or the other.

DAVID: You have indeed hit upon a crisis of evil for me in which none of the options seem moral. I have no reason to prefer the child's life to the mother's on the surface of it. I would indeed have to decide the matter in the situation but would not regard my action as a moral one in any case.

This is a crisis-of-evil situation for the rationalist.

GWEN: It's not obvious that postponing your decision until you are in the situation will make clearer what the basis for that decision ought to be. You also seem to take for granted that the taking of life is the moral issue. That's not quite accurate. You're not opposed to taking plant and animal life. Your sumptuous dinner last night made that clear. What you are concerned for is human life. But when does life count as human? You want to put it at the moment of conception. Why stop there? If someone were to argue that every egg should be fertilized, you would no doubt think that too extreme. Yet you maintain that every fertilized egg should be developed.

When does life count as human?

DAVID: That's not at all my contention. There are different requirements for developing a fertilized egg and for not terminating a human life.

GWEN: You're simply back to the omission-commission thing again. You can't carry the argument by taking for granted that the fertilized egg is a form of human life. The definition of human life is just the issue in question. No one doubts that the fetus is *potentially* human, but the issue is when does it become an *actual*

The point separating potential from actual human life is unclear.

human being. Roger says at viability, but it is not independent of its mother's care even at birth, nor has it completely achieved human form. Its nervous system, for instance, is still developing. There is no point at which one can draw a clear line and say that before a certain time this was only potentially a human being but after this it was actually one.

ROGER: Such considerations make it all the more expedient to attend to the rights of the woman carrying the fetus. Surely you agree, Gwen, that a woman owns her own body and as a result has a right to determine how it is treated.

Roger claims that a woman owns her body.

GWEN: We are back to where we began our discussion. You are still treating values in economic terms. You want to treat a person's body as a possession, as a storehouse for experiences, as a tool to do work.

ROGER: What alternative conception do you suggest?

GWEN: At least a different moral economy. The word "own," which we usually think of in terms of possession, also has appropriate uses in terms of responsibility. To own something is to take responsibility for it. The terms "own," "owe," and "ought" all have the same origin. I suppose the notion of responsibility is conceptually basic to that of possession.

ROGER: What does all this have to do with the abortion issue?

GWEN: I'm willing to say a woman owns her body if by that we mean she is responsible for it. A woman owns her actions too and the implications from them, even when they are not what she planned for or even expected. A man also owns his actions and their implications. If the interactions of a man and a woman result in pregnancy, then they are both responsible for—and in some sense responsible to—that product of their activity. The fetus within the mother is not a parasite attached to her body; it is an extension of herself. It is not an extension in the ways that some object of art is an extension of the artist, prized for what it is in itself. It is not an extension in the way that a hammer, say, is an extension of a carpenter, integrated with him as a tool and prized for the work it enables him to do. The fetus is an extension as a potential person for whom the mother bears responsibility directly proportional to its potentiality. She is most responsible in carrying it, less in nursing it, still less in nurturing it. She never ceases to own the child in the sense of being responsible to and for her, because the child, even when she has

Gwen claims that she is responsible for its welfare.

grown to womanhood, still exhibits potentialities that call upon a mother's responsibilities.

ROGER: Sounds like a highfalutin gobbledygook to me. When you bring all that responsibility talk into practice, how do you ever use it as a guide in making decisions? Have you ever performed an abortion?

GWEN: Yes, Roger, I've performed abortions, but I think my own views are more colored by my reflections on . . . well, on my own abortion. I'd be ashamed . . .

ROGER [interrupting]: I'm sorry, Gwen. I didn't mean to pry into your private life . . .

GWEN [interrupting in turn]: That's all right, Roger. It's important, I think, that you and David know how I justify abortion—and how I counsel the women or couples that ask me to perform an abortion for them.

It was for me a crisis of commitment. I had to weigh my obligations to my unborn child against other obligations. Knowing that its father had abandoned his responsibilities and knowing that the child would be deformed and retarded at birth weighed against my responsibilities to the child. Knowing that I would be better able than most—both financially and professionally—to care for such a child weighed in favor of maintaining my responsibility, at least through the child's early years. The limits the child would impose on my professional effectiveness and the limited fulfillment she could find in our society also were heavy considerations. In the end, I had to decide. My attitudes toward such a crisis of commitment are different from those David has toward a crisis of evil. I feel that I not only did the best that I could but I also feel I did the right thing.

Abortion may be seen as a crisis of commitment.

DAVID: But aren't you haunted by the thought that you might not have done the right thing?

GWEN: Sometimes, but that is one of the prices for being a fallible person having to maintain her integrity the best way that she can given her appraisal of her situation. If it's any consolation to you, I don't always think I have done the right thing, and I sometimes share your crisis of evil in which there doesn't seem to be a right thing to do.

The problem of self-doubt is a price of fallibility.

ROGER: For this issue, at least, David's basic thesis that there is no satisfactory out seems to have been sustained. He and I might both be inclined to be more charitable about your deliberative approach having seen how you applied it to an actual issue, but it still comes down to David's opposing abortion on demand, my favoring it, and your appraising specific conditions. Where does that leave us for effective decision making as a committee?

DAVID: It doesn't, it shouldn't, leave us with a relativistic attitude. It would be irresponsible to jump from the observation that coming to a common decision is difficult to the conclusion that it is impossible. Most appeals to relativism that I have heard amount to a moral cop-out. They produce the conceptual absurdity of an absolute relativism.

Differences in judgment shouldn't lead to relativism . . .

ROGER: What do you mean?

DAVID: If Gwen said, "Everything is relative," I would now take her to mean that everything is related to other things in some way or another. What most people mean by such a statement, however, is that nothing is related to anything, that there are no standards, that everything is arbitrary and capricious. It all comes down to "I'll believe what I believe, and you'll believe what you believe, and there's no way to come to an agreement or to change one another's minds." The results of such absolute relativism are that an individual cannot make sense of responsibility from one moment to another, even from decision to immediate action.

which means there are no standards . . .

ROGER: Why not?

DAVID: Because if there are no standards at all, then we could have nothing to measure the worth of his performance against from one time to the next. Just as there would be no standards to judge differences between individuals at any one time, there would be no standards to judge between a single individual's action at one time and that same individual's action at another. Under such circumstances, the very notion of judgment doesn't make sense. Once you admit standards for yourself, you open up the question of why these standards rather than others, and you are back to looking for a common basis for morality.

and which makes notion of judgment nonsensical.

ROGER: I don't think you can move so easily from the brink of the absurdity of absolute relativism to the safe ground of the pursuit of a common morality.

GWEN: Let me try. As David notes, I would always maintain that relative is always relative *to*. It may not imply turning the relative into an absolute. The relations might be mutually

Relatedness rests upon principles.

supportive and not require that we start with first principles. But the three of us do find ourselves driving relatives back to first principles; you, Roger, to a sense of sympathy and a discernment of enlightened self-interest, which undergird your greatest-happiness principle. This in turn becomes your principle for appraising what it means to be a moral being. Someone else may have a different appraisal but not an essentially different procedure for determining what her principles are. If she is able to make meaningful moral pronouncements at all, she must acknowledge moral principles as undergirding them.

ROGER: I'm not sure I find your argument more convincing than David's, but there seems no reason for us to talk about it further, since I don't think any of us is particularly inclined to the hazards of relativism that David describes.

GWEN: I find us each inclined to accent hazards to our moral deliberation that are most threatening to our own particular approach. David accents the hazards of relativism because they seem most likely to challenge his assertion of absolute rules. I seem most sensitive to the hazards of the cop-out of defining away moral problems. If you can rationalize an issue by defining it in such a way that it appears to present no challenge to your integrity, then you don't really have to deal with it as a moral issue. Although such defining away of issues appears to preserve integrity, it actually undercuts it by pretending things are other than they are.

The hazards of relativism challenge the assertion of absolute rules; the hazards of defining away moral problems challenge the assertion of integrity.

ROGER: If we pursue your thesis, Gwen, I suppose the most hazardous cop-out of my approach is to allow legal considerations to override moral considerations. It's often easy to excuse yourself from making moral decisions on the grounds that the issue has already been decided by law. So long as we recognize bad laws, inadequate laws, morally defective laws, we must preserve a sense of the moral as distinct from the legal.

The hazard of legal justifications is that they may override moral considerations.

DAVID: A hazard that the two of you have impressed me with is maintaining that inactivity is better than activity, that omission is better than commission. Part of the problem here is recognizing that the intention of the act involves responsibility for what is implied by the act and not just for what someone may think of as his purposes for the act. Conceived that way, the intentions for inactivity become as important as those for activity, and even the aim of some inactivity is exposed as avoiding moral responsibility. I still boldly proclaim "Sin boldly" when treating

Another hazard is preferring inactivity to activity.

a crisis of evil in the abstract, but I'm terribly tempted to retreat into "When in doubt, don't" when treating matters in the concrete.

GWEN: Each of us probably stands in danger of oversimplifying problems so that we can avoid difficult features and tailor the formulation of the problem to a ready solution based on the principles of one's own approach.

DAVID: We are equally prone to use complexities as an excuse for not coming to a principled decision in time for action.

GWEN: It is indeed hard to know in the abstract how such principled decisions will work out in the complexity of the concrete. It's the sort of problem that the existentialists used to characterize as the moment of truth. A friend of mine tells the story of how, when he was just out of med school and in residence for pediatrics, a mother brought her infant child into the emergency room. The child had stopped breathing some minutes before, and other bodily functions had stopped as well. My friend wavered momentarily, knowing that the fifteen minutes he supposed the child to have been without oxygen meant only a marginal survival possibility and almost certain brain damage.

All approaches share the problem of matching simple principles to complex situations.

DAVID: It will come as no surprise to either of you that I think he should do all he could to save the child's life.

ROGER: And it will be no surprise that I think he should not.

GWEN: Well, he did very quickly do mouth-to-mouth, heart palpitation, intravenous, and everything else he had been taught. He rationalized that it was a worthwhile exercise in practicing his art, if nothing else. Just when he was about to give up, the child began to revive. My friend paid the price for exercising his art of seeing that child every day in the hospital, existing in a state a little above that of a vegetable, for another year until it died.

Moral decisions may not always have satisfactory results.

DAVID: So, are you arguing that he shouldn't have saved the child's life?

GWEN: Well, this same friend also tells the story of a boy who had been hit by a car while playing in the street. His injuries had left him so damaged that after a day or so the neural surgeon on the case advocated that they pull the plugs on the support system that was the only basis for maintaining any sign of life. My friend argued—rather sentimentally, I think—that the boy had been out playing just the day before, as normal as any other boy; so surely they could wait another day before withdrawing the life-support system. Two weeks later, that boy was again out playing, as normal as any other boy.

DAVID: Which may contribute to the thesis that no genuinely moral decision is an easy one.

ROGER [going to the chalkboard again]: Even though we don't seem to be coming up with much in the way of positive policy, we do seem to have unfolded a long list of pitfalls. [Roger reads the list aloud as he writes]:

Hazards for Moral Deliberation
1. Making relativism absolute.
2. Using definitions to rationalize.
3. Using the legal to override the moral.
4. Preferring inactivity to activity.
5. Oversimplifying the issues.
6. Using the complexity of the issues to obscure action.

And I suppose the list can be extended.

GWEN: There certainly is a sense in which we agree about the foundations of moral decision. We are all agreed that moral decisions ought to be principled and that the base for the principles lies in human nature.

All participants agree that decisions should be principled . . .

DAVID: Yes. It's just that we can't agree on what human nature is. I think man is a rational animal. Roger seems to suppose he is a self-seeking animal, whose desires are mitigated by judgments of practical effects and sentiments of sympathetic concerns. You, Gwen, see humans as more complicated creatures who have characteristics and commitments not readily generalized for moral purposes apart from particular persons in specific situations.

but disagree on what human nature is.

ROGER: We may eventually come to some ultimate resolution to such weighty matters over our coffee breaks, but in the meantime we have to act on actual issues. Let's work for consensus, but we may have to resort to a majority vote for the greatest happiness for the greatest number.

As they turn from theory to practice . . .

[David is about to come back with a retort when a voice is heard over the loudspeaker.]

a real crisis arises . . .

VOICE: Dr Martin and Mr. Shepherd, report to the chief administrator's office; Dr. Martin and Mr. Shepherd, report to the chief administrator's office.

ROGER: Do you have any idea what this is about, Gwen?

GWEN: Do you remember the story I told last night about the conflict between the parents' religious obligation and my professional obligation? I didn't make the story up. I performed the operation yesterday afternoon.

that exposes an abstract example as an actual situation.

DAVID: Oh, my God! Does this amount to a criminal act?

ROGER: Probably not. Most of these cases are covered by tort law. It would be up to a judge to decide whose judgment was correct. The worst result is that someone would have to pay a financial settlement.

DAVID: Well, that's a kind of settlement of conflict that doesn't seem to fit into any of our senses of judgment.

ROGER: I'm pretty confident we can win this one on the grounds that any reasonable parent wants what is best for his child, and what Gwen did was clearly best for the child.

GWEN [already on her way out the door]: I hope this doesn't compromise the work of this committee. We were just getting squared away on the foundations aspect so that we could start to get some work done.

DAVID [under his breath as Roger and Gwen leave]: I'll pray for you both.

Questions for Reflection & Discussion

1. What does Gwen maintain that will keep her position from falling into narcissism (egoism) or into fascism (elitism)?

2. How does Roger avoid proliferation of conditions and exceptions to his rules in such a way that it keeps his rules from sliding to the level of a specific rule for each situation?

3. What is the tyranny of the majority? How, if at all, does this present a moral crisis for Roger's orientation? Why does Roger suppose this proves a virtue in the lifeboat example?

4. Why does Gwen claim that Roger's diagram favors his orientation? Does she succeed in constructing a scheme for the problems with Roger's position?

5. David claims Roger's position reduces the moral to the practical. Do you agree? Is that bad?

6. Gwen distinguishes consensus from majority and unanimity. Is

her consensus proposal likely to solve the lifeboat problem? Do you think this is a moral solution?

7. Are the disagreements over abortion among Roger, Gwen, and David simply disagreements over when a fetus becomes a human? If not, how do they reflect the basic differences in theoretical orientation?

8. Roger, in the end, lists a number of hazards for moral deliberation. If there are any you don't think hazardous, state why. If there are any you don't understand, attempt to state what confuses you about them. If there are other hazards you have discerned, what are they?

9. Gwen, in the end, claims that all three agree that moral decisions ought to be principled. What does she mean by that? Do they agree on this point? Do you agree? Why?

Bibliographical Notes

On COMPLETING HER reading of this dialogue, a student asked that I write a sequel so she could find out what happened to Gwen. Whatever your sense of the unresolved melodrama, it is clear that this dialogue does not offer a complete story about the conceptual foundations for moral decision, much less about implied resolutions to specific moral problems. At best it offers starting points for reflection and exploration of such matters. Perhaps the best I can offer here are some suggestions of where to begin such further inquiry, and, for that, I will begin with the dialogue itself.

Gwen, Roger, and David are not professional philosophers, nor even students of ethical theory. They all have some background in the liberal arts, and each may have had a course in ethics or moral philosophy as an undergraduate. Not one of them is a spokesperson for a particular moral philosopher, but as each attempts to develop a coherent theoretical perspective, he or she comes to champion a discernable ethical tradition. The position taken up by Roger is expressive of the *utilitarian* tradition, which received its classical formulation in John Stuart Mill's *Utilitarianism* (1863) in the nineteenth century, even though elements of the tradition can be traced as far back as ancient Greek thinkers, such as Epicurus (ca. 300 B.C.). The principle of enlightened self-interest is usually credited to Thomas Hobbes's *Leviathan*, the principle of sympathy to Adam Smith's *Theory of Moral Sentiments* (as well as the notion of an ideal, disinterested observer), and the principle of social utility to Jeremy Bentham's *An Introduction to the Principles of Morals and Leg-*

islation (1789). David takes a *deontological* position, accenting duty discerned by reason, as a base for his moral position. Because of Immanuel Kant's great influence, this position is sometimes called *Kantianism*. His *Foundations of the Metaphysics of Morals* (1785) is most frequently cited, though Kant's own wrestling with moral issues can be better viewed in his *Lectures on Ethics* (1790), and the relation of his ethical theory to other aspects of his thought can be seen in his *Critique of Practical Reason* (1788). Gwen's self-realization ethic finds its roots in ancient Greek thought, particularly Aristotle's *Nicomachian Ethics* (ca. 325 B.C.). Aristotle's view is sometimes called *eudaemonism*, from the Greek word meaning "good spirit," well-being, or flourishing. This tradition has continued through the medieval blending of Greek and Christian virtues and in such diverse "postmodern" thinkers as Hegel, Marx, and Nietzsche. The classical texts for these three traditions are available in print, many in a variety of editions, including paperback.

Each of these traditions finds able champions among professional moral philosophers today. While there is much disagreement over details, most present-day theorists show affinity for a utilitarian perspective, often to the point of taking it for granted. Richard Brandt's *A Theory of the Good and the Right* (New York: Oxford University Press, 1979)* exposes foundations for a utilitarian perspective in the light of recent psychology and social theory. A number of recent theorists have incorporated deontological elements into their theory, but Alan Donagan, in *The Theory of Morality* (Chicago: University of Chicago Press, 1979)*, offers a coherent duty-based theory that reflects not only Kantian kinds of rational foundations, but exposes a rich tradition that includes Thomistic, Stoic, and Biblical influences as well. Alastair MacIntyre, in *After Virtue* (Notre Dame, Ind.: University of Notre Dame Press, 1981)*, uses a historical methodology both to critique a current ethical theory and to invite a rethinking of moral matters along Aristotelean or Nietzschean lines. While there are a number of good, recent ethical treatises, these are perhaps the best exemplars of the three traditions exposed in this dialogue. Each offers enough of a critical exposition, not only of opponents, but of near relatives, to give a flavor of the current professional debates over the foundations of moral decision.

More accessible to beginners are texts written specifically for those who are not familiar with the historical traditions and debates. Two brief, single-author introductions are William Frankena, *Ethics* (Englewood Cliffs, N.J.: Prentice-Hall, 1963)*, and Robert Olson, *Ethics, A Short Introduction* (New York: Random House, 1978)*. More comprehensive and detailed, but still readable and accessible, is John Hospers, *Human Conduct* (New York: Harcourt, Brace & World, 1961)*. Richard Brandt, *Ethical Theory* (Englewood Cliffs, N.J.: Prentice-Hall, 1959)*

---

* The asterisk (*) here and following indicates that helpful bibliographies are included in the volume.

also gives a good critical review of major theories and issues. A text that focuses more on the reader as inquirer into moral issues is Bernard Rosen, *Strategies of Ethics* (Boston: Houghton Mifflin, 1978).

Selections on theoretical issues in ethics by both classical and modern thinkers have been collected in a number of anthologies. A chronological arrangement of readings can be found in A. I. Melden (ed.), *Ethical Theories* (Englewood Cliffs, N.J.: Prentice-Hall, 1955)*, and in Albert, Denise, and Peterfreund, *Great Traditions in Ethics*, 5th ed. (Belmont, Calif.: Wadsworth, 1984)*. Andrew Oldenquist, *Moral Philosophy* (Boston: Houghton Mifflin, 1984)* is another fine historical collection, which includes extensive introductions to the topically arranged theoretical issues; it is also keyed to the anthologized texts. Paul W. Taylor, *Problems of Moral Philosophy* (Belmont, Calif.: Wadsworth, 1978)*, and Philip Davis, *Introduction to Moral Philosophy* (Columbus, Ohio: Charles E. Merrill, 1973)* both offer a topical arrangement of selections.

For applying ethical principles to moral practice, there are a number of collections of essays on contemporary moral problems. Beginning students often have difficulty with these collections because the essays were originally written for professionals, not beginners. In an effort to avoid these difficulties, Vincent Barry, *Applied Ethics* (Belmont, Calif.: Wadsworth, 1978)* is written at an introductory level, but includes readings. In the first part, Barry outlines argument strategies and theoretical positions and problems. In the second part, he introduces the selected essays with background expositions on how the theories apply to a particular topic; and after the essays, "case presentations" focus more clearly on applying theoretical orientations to practical issues. A different approach to meeting the beginner's needs is that found in Tom Regan, *Matters of Life and Death* (New York: Random House, 1980), where each of the essays is an introduction to a specific topic written expressly for this volume by an expert in the field. Written for the beginner, the essays expose the relevant issues and appraise them from differing theoretical perspectives. Other good collections of essays on moral problems, but which lack the extensive aid to beginners found in the Barry and Regan texts, include James Rachels, *Moral Problems* (New York: Harper & Row, 1978), Jan Narveson (ed.), *Moral Issues* (New York: Oxford University Press, 1983), and Richard Wasserstrom, *Today's Moral Problems* (New York: Macmillan, 1975). These, and a number of other problems anthologies, offer good examples of current concerns, and they differ from one another more in arrangement and selection of specific essays than in quality and character of content.

Some recent anthologies on moral problems deserve special note: These are texts that treat moral issues against the thematic background of social, economic, and legal applications. James Sterba (ed.), *Morality in Practice* (Belmont, Calif.: Wadsworth, 1983)*, orders several topics of moral practice around problems of distribution of wealth and income, and shows in clear introductions how problems about one topic are interlaced with problems about the others. Each introduction is followed by an essay exposing basic concepts, several essays offering differing perspectives on the issues, and practical applications in judicial decisions on the issues. Other texts that juxtapose moral issues and public policy are Tom L. Beauchamp and Terry P. Pinkard (eds.), *Ethics and Public Policy* (Englewood Cliffs, N.J.: Prentice-Hall, 1983)*, Thomas A. Mappes and Jane S. Zembaty, *Social Ethics* (New York: McGraw-Hill, 1982)*, and Michael Bayles and Kenneth Henley, *Right Conduct* (New York: Random House, 1983). Beauchamp and Pinkard offer their own accessible introductory essays on issues related to freedom, justice, and respect for life, along with carefully matched pro-and-con written essays by others on specific issues. Mappes and Zembaty set the stage for their selected topics with introductory essays that key court decisions with philosophical debates. Bayles and Henley, after presenting selections of classical and recent theoretical statements, also introduce the essays on various moral problems with relevant court decisions.

The problems of relativism, emotivism, and intuitionism discussed in the first meeting of the dialogue are perhaps not so much parts of ethical theory as they are antecedents to it. These issues need sorting out before one can begin to think about what sort of foundations—if any—are possible. A classic on cultural relativism is E. Westermarck, *Ethical Relativity* (Paterson, N.J.: Littlefield, Adams & Co., 1960). Taylor's *Problems of Moral Philosophy* includes essays on cultural relativism, and Brandt's *Ethical Theory* offers a good discussion of the issues in Chapter 11. The issues of emotivism and intuitionism were much in debate in the first half of this century. These are now usually referred to as *metaethical* issues, having to do with the nature of moral discourse, and with its logical status, sources, and justifications. Many of the important papers from that early period are collected in Wilfrid Sellars and John Hospers (eds.), *Readings in Ethical Theory* (New York: Appleton-Century-Crofts, 1970). *Emotivism* is the belief that moral expressions basically are expressions of emotion, not judgments about the world. The version that has received most attention is Charles Stevenson, *Ethics and Language* (New Haven, Conn.: Yale University Press, 1943), and this gets critical scrutiny in J. O. Urmson, *The Emotive Theory of Ethics* (New York: Oxford University Press, 1968). Intuitionism proclaims that moral principles are in some sense known without critical reflection, often adding that critical evaluation and justification are not possible. G. E. Moore, *Principia Ethica* (Cambridge: Cambridge University Press, 1903), was chiefly responsible for generating much of the discussion on intuitionism in this century; W. D. Hudson, *Ethical Intuitionism* (London: Macmillan, 1967), puts these concerns into a broader historical context. Most of the anthologies on theoretical problems already mentioned give some attention to the metaethical issues of relativism, emotivism, and intuitionism.

The problems of freedom and moral responsibility discussed in the first meeting are also preliminary issues for ethical theory and have broader implications for the nature of human action and its relation to the natural order. There are many paperback collections of essays on the subject, but one of the best set of selections is in P. Edwards and A. Pap, *A Modern Introduction to Philosophy* (New York: Free Press, 1981)*. This book has a sixteen-page annotated bibliography by Edwards, which includes not only notes on the references, but also a conceptual ordering of the issues. You can also find good introductions to the issues of freedom and moral responsibility in J. Cornman and K. Lehrer, *Philosophical Problems and Arguments* (New York: Macmillan, 1974) and in Richard Taylor, *Metaphysics* (Englewood Cliffs, N.J.: Prentice-Hall, 1983). As suggested in the dialogue, views on moral responsibility often have great bearing on one's understanding of punishment. The above-cited books by Sterba, Barry, Regan, Bayles and Henley, Mappes and Zembaty, and Beauchamp and Pinkard all have good sections on punishment, usually with a focus on capital punishment.

In the dialogue, issues of justice and human rights receive only marginal attention in the discussion of the relation of ethics to law, during the third meeting. But for many theorists, these issues are central and basic. Sterba, Beauchamp and Pinkard, and Bayles and Henley all offer essays in their anthologies that expose theoretical perspectives, and Regan, in *Matters of Life and Death*, has a helpful introductory essay on issues of justice and rights. *Libertarianism* is the perspective that gives priority to individual liberties when considering the questions of social justice and welfare. This position is set forth and defended in John Hospers, *Libertarianism* (Los Angeles: Nash, 1971), and in Robert Nozick, *Anarchy, State and Utopia* (New York: Basic Books, 1974). It is usually set in opposition to *socialism,* the contention that social regulation provides the best basis for justice and human rights. For a non-Marxist perspective on socialism, see Michael Harrington, *Socialism* (New York: Bantam Books, 1970); for a Marxist perspective, see Milton Fisk, *Ethics and Society: A Marxist Interpretation of Value* (New York: New York University Press, 1980). Other theorists have tried to work out positions somewhere between these poles. The most noteworthy recent effort is John Rawls, *A Theory of Justice* (Cambridge: Harvard University Press, 1971). James Sterba, *Justice: Alternative Political Perspectives* (Belmont, Calif.: Wadsworth, 1980), is a good presentation of rival viewpoints.

It is important to remember that perspectives on social and legal issues are distinct from the foundations for those perspectives. Nozick grounds his libertarian views in his understanding of natural rights, and a social contract view serves as the foundation for Rawls's position on social welfare. The contractual ground does not imply the welfare perspective, however. Many contractarians are libertarians (including Hospers), and some social welfare notions are grounded in conceptions of natural rights. In our dialogue, David is an advocate of both natural rights and natural law, but he's interested in social welfare, while Roger, who is clearly arguing for a contractarian position in issues of laws and rights, is just as clearly a libertarian. Foundations for social perspectives are closely related to foundations of law. Martin Golding (ed.), *The Nature of Law* (New York: Random House, 1966), and Ronald Dworkin (ed.), *The Philosophy of Law* (New York: Oxford University Press, 1977) present a number of recent essays on the foundations of law.

It is clear in the dialogue that David's understandings of natural law and natural rights are motivated by religious as well as philosophical considerations. His conclusions are influenced not only by Thomas Aquinas and Immanuel Kant, but also by H. Emil Brunner, *The Divine Imperative* (Philadelphia: Westminster, 1947), and by Dietrich Bonhoeffer, *Ethics* (New York: Macmillan, 1955). It may also be clear that David's reliance on these sources is neither coherent nor coercive, philosophically. Many ethical theorists agree with Roger that religion requires *that* you be moral, but does not favor one particular foundation for moral decision. Edward Long, *A Survey of Christian Ethics* (New York: Oxford University Press, 1967) gives an account of the ethical foundations appealed to by Catholic and Protestant Christians. P. T. Jersild and D. A. Johnson, *Moral Issues and Christian Response* (New York: Holt, Rinehart & Winston, 1976) gives examples of differing perspectives and applications to current moral issues.

Beginning students can find still another set of starting points for further inquiry in Paul Edwards (ed.), *Encyclopedia of Philosophy* (New York: Macmillan, 1967). There are two survey articles on ethics: R. Abelson and K. Nielson, "Ethics, History of" (vol. 3, p. 81), and K. Nielson, "Ethics, Problems of" (vol. 3, p. 117). In addition, a whole range of articles on moral decision and ethical theory are placed under the "Ethics" heading.

Where you go in your reading after this dialogue will largely be determined by your interests and resources. No matter where you begin, you will likely be led by your own critical reflection, into other areas. As Gwen, David, and Roger made clear, the issues and problems are not unrelated; and you, like they, will probably find yourself moving from one to another as you reflect on the foundations of moral decisions.